NUMBER
GAMES
TO IMPROVE
YOUR
CHILD'S
ARITHMETIC

ABRAHAM B. HURWITZ
ARTHUR GODDARD
DAVID T. EPSTEIN

NUMBER GAMES TO IMPROVE YOUR CHILD'S ARITHMETIC

FUNK & WAGNALLS
NEW YORK

Book design & illustrations by the
Whole Works: Chas. Peach, Cathy
Rennich & Ethel Steginsky

Manufactured in the United States of
America

ISBN 0-308-10162-6

Library of Congress Cataloging in Publication Data

Hurwitz, Abraham B.
    Number games to improve your child's arithmetic.

    Includes index.
    1. Mathematical recreations. 2. Arithmetic – Study
and teaching. I. Epstein, David T., joint author.
II. Goddard, Arthur, joint author. III. Title.
QA95.H89 1975   793.7'4   74-23849
ISBN 0-308-10162-6

1 2 3 4 5 6 7 8 9 10

TO THE YOUNGER GENERATION,
who, we hope, will now derive as much pleasure
from arithmetic as from the other two of the three R's

CONTENTS

PART ONE: TO THE PARENT

1 What This Book Can Do for Your Child   2

2 What These Games Teach   5

3 How to Use This Book   7

PART TWO: GAMES TO PLAY

4 Easy Games for the Young Child   16

    Color Me   16

    Color Me Sad   17

    Color Me Mad   19

    Count and Connect   19

    Write Connections   21

    Follow the Numbers   22

    Count Down   24

    I've Got Your Number!   25

    Target 15   26

    Pitch or Snap   27

    Pitch and Toss   28

    Numbered Daze   29

	Cross Out	30
	Number Twirl	31
	Trial and Error	33
5	Oral Games	34
	Number, Please	34
	Buzz	36
	Umpty-Um Buzz	38
	Hippety-Hop Buzz	38
	Make It	38
	Coin Count	39
	Handy Figures	40
	Snatch Match	41
	Snatch-a-Batch	42
	What's the Difference?	43
	Finger Figures	44
	Digital Computer	45
	Finger Shoot	46
	Gazintas	46
6	Paper-and-Pencil Games	48
	Number Maze	48
	Arithme-Tic-Tac-Toe	50
	Crisscross	51
	Number Row	53
	Configurations	53
	Product Net	55
	Square Accounts	56
	Imprisoned Numbers	59
7	Card Games	61
	Some Sums!	61
	Sum Building	63
	Pyramid	63
	Sam Pyramid	66
	Mads Pyramid	66
	Tic-Tac Bingo	67
	War	68

Mads War 69

Fraction War 70

Fraction Blackjack 72

Flip-Count 73

Give and Take 74

Table Numbers 75

Add-Joining Cards 77

29 Game 78

Target 31 80

Multisum 82

Sets and Sequences 83

Sad Casino 85

Casino Baseball 88

Baseball Mads 89

Concentration 91

8 Games with Dice and Dominoes 93

Precise Dice 93

Fireman up the Ladder 94

Trail Blazing 96

Math Path 98

The Snake 98

Sink the Ship 102

Locus-Pocus 104

Golf 107

Contact 110

Factor Extractor 112

Fraction Extraction 113

Decimal Designs 113

Banker 114

Poker Dice 115

Six Clicks 116

Won by One 118

Use Twos 119

Mads Dominoes 119

High-Low 121

9 Games with Prepared Materials   123
    Figure It Out   123
    Line-Up   126
    Exact Reckoning   128
    Exact Weight   129
    Exact Measure   130
    Combinations   131
    Tag   132
    Divisor Deviser   133
    Factor Hockey   135
    Drop It!   138
10 Party Games   141
    Giant Step   141
    A-Rhythm-e-Tag   143
    Back Numbers   145
    Marble Pitch   145
    Coin Toss   147
    Number-Ring Toss   148
    Stand Up and Be Counted   150
    Divide and Conquer   153
    Boxing Match   154
    Unboxing Match   156
    Batter Up!   157
    What's My Number?   158
    Your Number's Up!   160
    Sum Bingo   161
    Mads Bingo   162
    A-Lotto-Numbers   163

PART THREE: FIGURES FAST AND FUNNY
11 Arithmetricks   166
    Sum Speed   166
    Sum Mystery   168
    Psychic Arithmetic   170
    Odds and Evens   171

Odd or Even?   172
Division Precision   173
The Case of the Missing Number   174
The Exact Card   175
The Precise Word   176
What Are the Odds?   178
Addition Magician   179
12 Shortcuts in Arithmetic   181
13 Oddities of Arithmetic   195
14 Quips and Jests   210

PART FOUR: APPENDIX
The Language of Arithmetic   222
Table of Equivalents   226
Other Books of Mathematical Games   228
Commercially Available Arithmetic Games   230

Index of Skills Taught   237
Index of Games   243

NUMBER
GAMES
TO IMPROVE
YOUR
CHILD'S
ARITHMETIC

PART ONE:
TO THE PARENT

1

WHAT THIS BOOK CAN DO FOR YOUR CHILD

This book provides a carefully selected and thoroughly tested set of educational games at the elementary level that your child can play with you, with his friends, or by himself, to help him master the basic skills of arithmetic.

No longer need the learning of addition, subtraction, multiplication, and division be a tedious chore to be approached with loathing and dread. On the contrary, playing these games can arouse in your child a desire to learn and can give him an easy and pleasant way of practicing the fundamental techniques of counting and calculation. Your child's curiosity will be stimulated, and he will develop enthusiasm for further learning.

At the same time, the games in this book can, by indirection, make him eager to think, to concentrate on fascinating problems, to imagine solutions, to observe numerical and quantitative relationships, and to perform arithmetical operations with accuracy and speed.

As he plays one game after another or different variations of the same game, he will also be reviewing, without strain, all the skills needed for proficiency in arithmetic. The pleasurable experience and anticipation associated with these games are conducive to learning and will render it more effective and long-lasting.

In short, these games not only *motivate* learning but also *enrich* it. The emphasis at all times is on *play*—on activities accompanied by the pleasures of competition, suspense, surprise, and reward, as well as the satisfaction that comes from success and the child's growing sense of mastery. This is the way to build his confidence in his intellectual powers and to encourage him to further effort. Played over a period of years, these games can do more than lay the foundation for a practical knowledge of mathematics; they also can help to develop a lifelong love of the subject.

Thus *Number Games to Improve Your Child's Arithmetic* is neither a textbook of arithmetic nor a collection of puzzles that, once solved, have served their transient purpose of entertaining and can hold no further interest for the child.

On the contrary, each game in this book can become the starting point of an endless series of possible "plays," including variations, refinements, and complications that challenge the ingenuity and resourcefulness of the participants. There are hardly any limits—except those of the players' time, patience, and inventiveness—to the myriad "moves" that can be made in any game.

Paralleling the wealth of possible variations in each game is the wide diversity in the techniques of play.

Your child need never be bored. There are verbal games, games that emphasize quickness of response, paper-and-pencil games, card games, domino games, dice games, and others that elude any precise classification.

In sum, this book is an invitation to a lifetime of joyful discovery and adventure in the realm of numbers. It is the playway to learning arithmetic.

2

WHAT THESE GAMES TEACH

The essential purpose of this book is to help you to teach your school-age child the basic concepts, principles, and skills of arithmetic.

Such knowledge has obvious value for everyone. We live in a world of numbers. An elementary familiarity with the operations of arithmetic is indispensable to carrying out such practical tasks of daily life as counting change, keeping records of purchases and sales, reading the temperature, telling time, balancing a checking account, planning a budget, or computing interest on money in the bank.

Small wonder, then, that a knowledge and love of arithmetic is one of the greatest assets you can give your child! As Plato said, "Every person should learn this art early in life. Just as every child is taught the alphabet, so he should learn calculation as a form of amusement."

This is precisely what the games in this book have been designed to accomplish. They are not intended to provide practice in the specialized techniques of what is today called "the New Math."

In this respect, these games are an educational substitute for time-wasting forms of recreation. When your child plays a game of checkers, dice, dominoes, bingo, lotto, or cards as adapted here, or any other game in this book, he will be developing proficiency in counting, adding, subtracting, multiplying, dividing, making numerical comparisons and distinctions, and calculating — not only with whole numbers but with decimals and fractions. Moreover, he will learn how to perform these operations rapidly as well as accurately with the aid of shortcuts.

3

HOW TO USE THIS BOOK

Most of the games in this book are intended to be played first in the intimacy of your home, by the child alone or with you or members of the immediate family. A separate chapter has been devoted to party games for larger groups of children.

To keep the emphasis on fun and recreation, and to let the learning take care of itself, as it surely will, another chapter consists of what we call "arithmetricks." These games can be used to arouse interest at the outset or to overcome negative attitudes of fear or dislike that your child may have developed toward arithmetic. By using the "arithmetricks," you can entice him into a game or just set the mood of relaxation. Still another chapter is composed of mathematical oddities, "teasers," stunts, and novelties, as well as jokes and riddles, to stimulate your child's interest.

In addition, every child — and especially the child who has been having trouble with arithmetic — will welcome the many shortcuts to be found in the chapter devoted to these useful timesaving devices. Having at his command a quick and easy way to perform operations that once were looked upon as a chore or a bore will give your child a sense of power and inspire him with confidence in his ability to handle arithmetic problems.

You should, then, have no difficulty in interesting your child in these games. Children enjoy winning a contest. They derive satisfaction from using a set of clues to work out the solution of a problem. They take pleasure both in sharing their knowledge and skills with their friends and in outwitting them. They rise to a challenge and take pride in their ability to meet it.

Your educational role as a parent using this book is essentially *motivational* and *supportive*. You will help your child, at first, to select the games to be played, interest him in them, introduce them to him, play some of them with him, and encourage him with your help and praise. At the same time, you will have the opportunity of sharing in his exploration and discovery of the wondrous world of numbers.

SELECTING THE GAMES

The sequence in which these games are to be played depends entirely on the level of ability of your child, his rate of progress, and his interests. The art of guidance here lies in selecting the right game that will interest him at the moment, teaching him the principle or skill that he needs to learn, and stimulating him to proceed on his own to other games or variations in ever mounting spirals of aspiration and proficiency.

You will therefore want to take into consideration the following factors for each game:

1. skills taught
2. materials needed
3. number of players
4. method of play

The information about each of these factors is readily available for every game.

SKILLS TAUGHT

The skills taught by each game are listed under its title. For example, under the heading "Buzz," the skills listed are counting, multiplication, and division.

In addition, the Index of Skills Taught (see the Appendix) will enable you to locate at a glance just the game you need to correct your child's weaknesses, to reinforce previous learning, or to extend his arithmetical abilities into new areas, such as fractions and decimals.

Incidentally, throughout the book we have used the expression "Mads" as a shorthand designation for the four fundamental operations of arithmetic — multiplication, addition, division, and subtraction. These are the basic skills taught in the games in this book.

MATERIALS NEEDED

Each game has been devised to be readily playable. A minimum of preparation by the parent or the child is required. Indeed, for most of the games in Chapter 4 and Chapter 5, you will need no material at all.

Whatever materials may be needed are easy to find or produce. Many of these games have been adapted from those which your child no doubt already knows and enjoys playing, like bingo, lotto, casino, and dominoes. To give these familiar recreational activities an instructive purpose and value, you may need to prepare or have available certain materials.

Chapter 6 consists wholly of paper-and-pencil games. If graph paper is needed for any of them, you will find that information under the title of the game.

Ordinary playing cards are the only materials needed for playing the games in Chapter 7.

Either dominoes or dice, as specified under the title in each case, are needed for playing the games grouped together in Chapter 8.

Games that require you to prepare materials are found chiefly in Chapter 9, though a few are also included in Chapter 4. Naturally, you will want to have these materials ready in advance. You will find them specified under the title of each game.

If the materials called for are cards prepared with numbers, signs, or examples, a simple method of producing them is to take an old deck of playing cards and paste on the front of each card a detachable sticker on which the necessary notation can be printed with a felt-tipped marking pen. (Ideal for this purpose are self-adhesive file-folder labels.)

Another method of preparing for such a game is to use three-inch by five-inch cards cut up into one-inch squares on each of which a number, symbol, or example can be placed. Out of fifteen such cards you can make 225 squares. In the directions for playing each game with prepared cards, you will find exact information concerning the number of cards required and the notation to place on each card.

In some of the games it has been suggested that a time limit be set for each answer in order to encourage speedy responses. The word "timer" has been included in such cases among the materials listed under the title. Your timer can be a wrist watch, a stop watch, a clock, a disk bell, an hourglass egg timer, a gong, or an electric timer such as is used for cooking.

NUMBER OF PLAYERS

Some of these games are for one player only. Others can be played by just two. Still others may be played by three or more or are best played with large groups.

You can see just how many players each game is suited for by glancing at this information under its title.

METHOD OF PLAY

For each game and its subsequent variations the method of play is described step by step. Before introducing a game to your child, first read the description of it yourself and become familiar with its possible variations. Next, prepare your materials, if any are needed. Then, name the game and explain slowly and clearly as much of it as is needed to begin playing. Keep the rules brief at first, and add other rules and complications as the game progresses, after your child has mastered its basic pattern.

It is a good idea to join in the game yourself, at least at the beginning. Your participation and enthusiasm can hardly fail to prove infectious. But if the child prefers to play by himself or with his peers, you may reduce your role to that of umpire or scorekeeper, or you may delegate the job to an older child in the group under your supervision.

Praise the child for his successful efforts. Remind him of past successes if he tends to become discouraged. If he fails to arrive at the correct answer, tell him what it is, show him how it is calculated, and continue with the game. If you correct his mistakes promptly and kindly, and if you answer his questions simply, clearly, and patiently, your child will learn rapidly, and you will build a close, warm relationship with him conducive to continued progress.

LEVEL OF MATURITY

All the games in this volume are designed to be played by children ranging from the primary grades to the sixth grade of elementary school. It is not possible to describe the level of maturity of any particular game in terms of the precise age for which it is suitable. Children of the same age differ widely in their ability to handle numbers. Besides, as you will discover, a game that may appear challenging or difficult to an eleven-year-old can prove easy for a child of eight. Because children even in the same grade of school differ too widely in ability to fit neatly into any exactly limited bracket of intellectual maturity or mathematical ability, you must discover from experience just where your child is to be placed. You will then have the pleasure of watching him advance from one level to the next as he gains skill through playing the games.

Naturally, a game should not be so difficult for your child that he will be frustrated in his effort to meet its challenge, nor should it be so easy that he will find it boring. In any case, you will generally find it possible to adjust the difficulty of a particular game to the individual needs of your child. You can make it easier by relaxing its rules or by using small whole numbers as examples; and you can make a game harder by following the suggestions we have included in virtually every game.

Moreover, the variations supplied for many of the games offer still another means of graduating the difficulty of the intellectual challenge. It is advisable to begin by playing the first game in a series before trying any of its variations. You can then simplify or complicate the game to adapt it to any degree of mathematical aptitude or any level of intelligence.

To aid you in beginning, we have provided in the fourth chapter, "Easy Games for the Young Child," a number of simple games that constitute what educators call a "readiness" program for the child in the primary grades or for the beginner. These are the most elementary games in the book. But even these have variations that permit them to be escalated gradually to more challenging heights.

The games suitable for the broadest range of abilities are generally those we have included in the chapter entitled "Party Games." These can be best played in large families or classes.

OTHER AIDS

For your convenience, you will find in the Appendix the Index of Skills Taught and a number of additional aids.

The Table of Equivalents should prove helpful in playing or preparing for any game calling for the child to match or think of equivalent values in the measurement of intervals of time, areas and volumes of space, or weights of masses. The text describing such games makes a reference to this table.

A glossary, The Language of Arithmetic, has been included in the Appendix to familiarize the child with the terminology and symbols commonly employed in arithmetic. Occasional references to this glossary will be found in the text.

If you wish to pursue the subject of this book further, you will find additional literature on it listed in the annotated bibliography entitled Other Books of Mathematical Games.

Finally, a list of commercially produced games with numbers has been included as a supplement to those described in this book.

PART TWO:
GAMES TO PLAY

4

EASY GAMES FOR THE YOUNG CHILD

Although many of the games in the following chapters are also suitable for children in the elementary grades, we have grouped here an assortment particularly appropriate for youngsters just beginning to find their way in the world of numbers.

Some of these games are oral; some are played with dominoes or dice; some require playing cards; some use paper and pencil; some need prepared materials; and some just involve physical activities such as turning, pulling, jumping, pointing, running, tagging, or pitching coins.

COLOR ME

RECOGNITION OF NUMERALS
Two or more players   Dice
Paper and pencil   Crayons

Each player draws or traces on his paper the figure shown on page 18.

Then the players take turns rolling the dice. Each player must color the part of the figure that bears the number he turns up. If a player rolls a number that he has already turned up, he loses his chance, and the next player rolls the dice.

The winner is the one who first completely colors his figure.

COLOR ME SAD

SUBTRACTION, ADDITION, DIVISION

Two or more players   Crayons
Set of cards   Paper and pencil

The figure in this variation of Color Me is colored SAD because each card has a problem in Subtraction, Addition, or Division to which the answer is a number on a part of the figure to be colored.

Here are a few examples:
Subtraction: $8 - 5, 12 - 8, 7 - 2$, etc.
Addition: $8 + 4, 6 + 3, 9 + 2$, etc.
Division: $10 \div 2, 9 \div 3, 8 \div 4, 12 \div 6$, etc.

The cards bearing the examples are placed face down on the table. Then the players take turns drawing a card, solving the problem, and coloring the appropriate part on their respective figures. The first to complete coloring his figure is the winner.

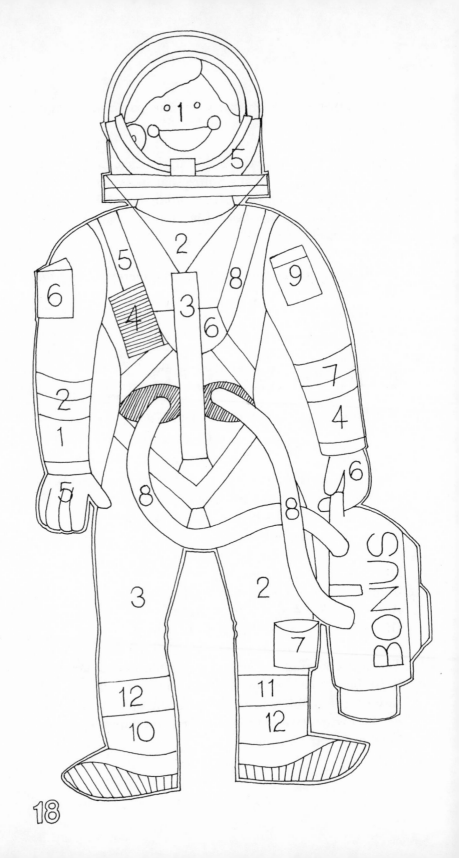

18

COLOR ME MAD

MULTIPLICATION, ADDITION, DIVISION

Two or more players   Dice
Set of cards   Crayons
Paper and pencil

The figure in this variation of Color Me is colored MAD because each card has a problem in Multiplication, Addition, or Division to which the answer is a number on a part of the figure to be colored. It is therefore necessary to insert in the figure larger numbers, up to 36.

Instead of a set of cards with problems, the players can roll dice. In that case, they are free to multiply, add, or divide in order to get a number matching one in an area of the figure that still needs to be colored.

COUNT AND CONNECT

COUNTING BY ONES, TWOS, THREES, FOURS, AND FIVES; MULTIPLICATION

One or more players   Paper
Colored pencils

Write all the numbers from 1 through 15 at random on a large sheet of paper, as illustrated.

In the simplest form of this game, the player counts out loud as he connects the numbers in proper sequence with a crayon or colored pencil.

If he makes no error, he counts by twos, using a crayon or pencil of another color to connect the numbers. Then he counts by threes, fours, and fives, each time using a different color to make the connections.

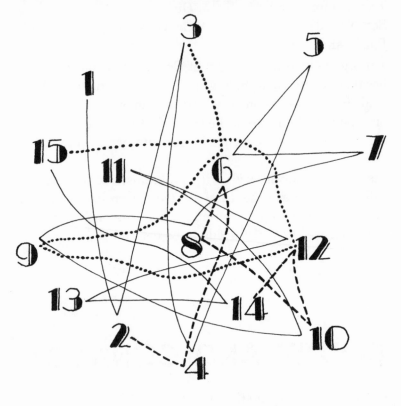

——————————— (or red) Counting by 1s
– – – – – – – – – (or blue) Counting by 2s
··················· (or green) Counting by 3s

If two or more play, each one can make up a chart with numbers for the other to connect, and different numbers may be used. The object of the game is to see which player can complete his chart more accurately or more quickly than the others.

WRITE CONNECTIONS

COUNTING BY ONES, TWOS, THREES, FOURS, ETC.; MULTIPLICATION

One or more players   Paper and pencil
Ruler   Colored crayons

With a compass or a paper plate, make a large circle. Mark it off clockwise with the numbers from 1 through 24, evenly spaced.

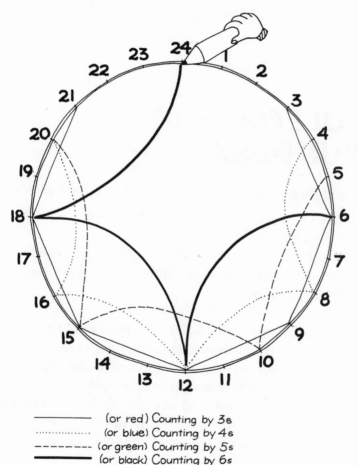

——————— (or red) Counting by 3s
················ (or blue) Counting by 4s
– – – – – – – (or green) Counting by 5s
━━━━━━━ (or black) Counting by 6s

This game is a variation of Count and Connect and proceeds in the same way. Each player, in turn, counts out loud as he connects the numbers in proper sequence with the help of a ruler and a crayon or colored pencil. At first, the player counts by ones, then by twos, next by threes, and so on, each time connecting the numbers with a differently colored crayon.

After several rounds, the numbers can be raised. With even higher numbers the multiplication table can be extended indefinitely.

FOLLOW THE NUMBERS

ODD, EVEN, AND PRIME NUMBERS; ADDITION
One or two players   Graph paper
Colored crayons
Insert the numbers 0 through 9 ten times at random in the hundred boxes of a square consisting of ten boxes on each side, as shown.

The player must first "follow the numbers" by finding his way from the entrance, at one corner, to the center of the square, moving only to connecting boxes containing even numbers. He traces his route with a pencil or a crayon. Then he must find his way from the center to the exit at the opposite corner by moving only to connecting boxes containing an odd number, as illustrated here.

2	9	6	2	8	5	5	0	7	9
3	4	8	2	7	2	4	5	6	6
1	6	1	6	6	9	4	1	2	3
0	6	9	4	2	0	8	7	6	2
8	2	3	8	9	2	8	6	5	4
1	7	3	3	5	1	4	9	4	7
9	5	4	4	9	7	3	2	5	8
8	3	6	5	8	2	8	7	6	7
6	4	8	6	4	3	7	9	3	0
1	2	7	9	3	1	7	5	9	1

Next, the player must draw a line surrounding every two or three numbers that add up to fifteen as long as the boxes containing these numbers are adjacent. Any sum between ten and twenty can be chosen, or three, four, or five numbers can be linked together to form a chain adding up to the required total.

When this game is played by two, each uses a differently colored crayon. Each player prepares a box for the other and gives him a problem to solve—for example, moving only to prime numbers (see The Language of Arithmetic, in the Appendix) or connecting numbers that are contiguous to add up to a given sum.

Each correct solution counts one point. Each error costs the player who makes it two points.

COUNT DOWN

COUNTING BY ONES, TWOS, AND THREES;
ADDITION

Two or more players   Playing cards

The first player, after shuffling the cards, places the deck facedown and turns up from the top one card at a time. Meanwhile, he counts by ones up to thirteen: 1, 2, 3, 4, 5, 6, 7, 8, 9, 10, 11, 12, 13. If the number on the card he turns up corresponds to the number he is calling out as he counts, he removes the card from the deck and continues counting from where he left off, until all fifty-two cards have been turned up—that is, through four complete runs of from 1 to 13. (For this game, the king counts as 13; the queen, as 12; and the jack, as 11.) The player then scores the sum of the cards he has removed. Thus, if he removed 3, 5, and 10, his score for the round is $3 + 5 + 10 = 18$.

Each player follows the same procedure when his turn comes, always starting, of course, with a full deck. After all have had a chance, the player with the highest score wins the round.

For the second round, the kings must be removed from the deck. Now each player, in turn, counts to twelve by twos: 2, 4, 6, 8, 10, 12, through eight complete runs, turning up cards at the same time. Cards with numbers that are turned up when they are called out in the counting are removed, as before, and scored by being summed up, as in the first round.

For the third and final round of the match, keep the kings out of the deck. This time, count by threes to twelve: 3, 6, 9, 12, through twelve runs. In all other respects, the game should be played as in the first two rounds.

The winner of the match is the player with the highest total score from all three rounds.

I'VE GOT YOUR NUMBER!

ADDITION, SUBTRACTION, MULTIPLICATION, DIVISION, DISTINGUISHING BETWEEN GREATER AND LESS, DISTINGUISHING BETWEEN ODD AND EVEN

Two or more players   Paper and pencil

Cupping his hand to hide his writing, the first player writes any number from 1 to 10.

The other players now take turns trying to guess the secret number by asking the first player questions that require him to perform addition, subtraction, multiplication, or division, or to distinguish between odd and even and between greater and less. For example, players may ask questions like: Is your number greater than 3×2? Is your number less than half of 10? Can your number be divided by 2? Is your number less than the difference between 8 and 4?

The first player must answer correctly and must show his number if any of his opponents guesses correctly.

The player who guesses the secret number with the fewest questions wins the round.

If the player to whom a question is addressed answers incorrectly, his questioner gets credit for one question fewer.

In later rounds, larger numbers can be used.

TARGET 15

ADDITION

Two or more players   Playing cards

For this game, each picture card will count as 5. After shuffling the cards, place them facedown on the table.

The first player draws three cards, one at a time, and tries to make the sum of 15 by adding their numerical values. If he succeeds, he places his cards to one side for his collection. If he is unsuccessful, he turns over and discards the unused cards.

The players take turns until all the cards in the deck are used up. Each card collected counts one point. The winner is the player with the most points after an agreed number of rounds or the player who first scores twenty-five points.

PITCH OR SNAP

ADDITION, MULTIPLICATION,
ROMAN NUMERALS

Two or more players   Chalk or pencil
Coins

Draw with a pencil on a sheet of paper or chalk on the sidewalk the design shown. Adapt the size of the design to the coin to be used in tossing.

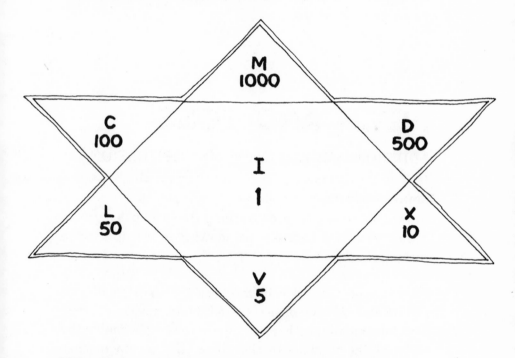

If the design is laid on a table, the players snap the coins from its edge; otherwise, they snap the coins from a designated distance on the pavement.

The players take turns pitching the coins. If a coin enters a box without touching the boundary line, the player who tossed it scores the value of the number in the box.

The game can be made more difficult if the value of the coin is multiplied by that of the number in the box. In that case, begin with pennies and then use nickels and dimes. For example, if a nickel lands in the box with the number 5, the score is $5 \times 5 = 25$.

A variation would use only Roman numerals in the diagram.

PITCH AND TOSS

ADDITION, SUBTRACTION, MULTIPLICATION
Two or more players   Chalk or pencil
Coins, bottle caps, or checkers

In this variation of Pitch or Snap the design consists of circles within a triangle, as shown, with a number in each circle.

Each player snaps a coin or checker or bottle cap onto the design. If the object tossed lands inside a circle without touching its border, the player scores double the value of the number in the circle. If the coin touches borders—say, those of the circles enclosing 4, 5, and 8—the player scores the sum of these numbers, in this case, 17.

The game can be made more interesting if plus or minus signs are inserted before the numbers so that the players

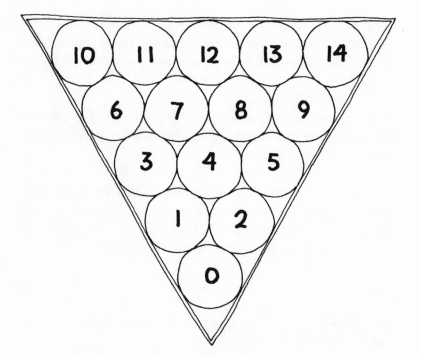

can have practice in addition, subtraction, or even multiplication.

NUMBERED DAZE

ADDITION, MULTIPLICATION

Two or more players   Calendar
Coins or bottle caps

The days that are numbered in this variation of Pitch or Snap are those of an old calendar. Just tear off a sheet of any month with thirty-one days and place it on the floor.

The players take turns tossing or snapping coins onto the calendar. Each player scores the value of the number in the box into which his coin lands without touching an edge.

After a few rounds, scores may be calculated by adding the values of the numbers in the boxes whose borders a coin touches.

Once again, if coins of different values are used, the denomination of the coin can be multiplied by the numerical value in the box in which it lands. Thus, if a dime lands in box 14, the player scores 140.

CROSS OUT

ADDITION, MULTIPLICATION
Two, three, or four players   Dice
Playing cards   Paper and pencil
Each player writes on his own sheet of paper the numbers 2 through 12.

The first player rolls the dice, adds the two numbers turned up — say, 6 + 3 — and crosses out on his paper the number equivalent to their sum, in this case, 9. He continues in this way until the sum of the numbers he rolls is the same as a number already crossed out on his paper — for example, 5 + 4 = 9.

It then becomes the next player's turn to roll the dice and proceed similarly. The game continues in this fashion until one player has crossed out all his numbers.

Instead of writing down numbers, each child could lay face up on the table playing cards with the values 2, 3, 4, 5, 6, 7, 8, 9, 10, 11 (jack), and 12 (queen). He could then turn over the card with the numerical value equal to the sum of the numbers he rolls. The player who turns over all his cards first wins.

By way of variation, the numbers crossed out can be equivalent to the products of the numbers appearing on the dice when they are rolled. In that case, each player should write on his paper the following numbers: 1, 2, 3, 4, 5, 6, 8, 9, 10, 12, 15, 16, 18, 20, 24, 25, 30, 36 — a total of eighteen numbers. Thus, if a player rolls a 6 and a 3, he must cross out their product ($6 \times 3 = 18$).

If playing cards are used, each of four players turns up the cards in a suit from 2 through 12 (queen) and then turns over any cards whose numbers he rolls with the dice, until one player turns over all his cards. He is the winner.

NUMBER TWIRL

ADDITION, MULTIPLICATION, DECIMALS

Two or more players   Paper plate
Paper clip   Pin

This is a game of chance. Although much depends on luck, skill in arithmetic is also essential for success.

First make a number wheel by writing the digits from 1 through 9 clockwise around the outer rim of a paper

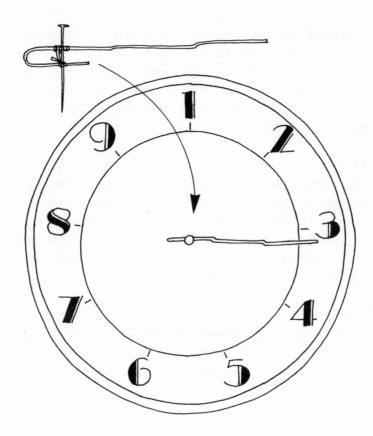

plate, as shown. Stick a pin through the center, and over this slip a paper clip straightened to form a pointer.

Each player, in turn, gets two spins. He takes the numbers that the spinner stops closest to and first adds them, then multiplies them, and finally adds the results of the two operations to get his score. For example, the numbers 6 and 4 add up to 10 and have 24 as their product, so that the score would be 34 altogether.

The player attaining the highest score after each has had ten rounds wins the game.

After several rounds have been played, the spaces between the numbers can be divided into decimals: 1, 1.25, 1.5, 1.75, 2.0, 2.25, etc. At first the score should be arrived at just by adding the two figures; with practice, the multiplication of decimals can be included.

TRIAL AND ERROR

ADDITION, SUBTRACTION, MULTIPLICATION, DIVISION

Two or more players   Paper and pencil
One die   Timer

Each player, in turn, rolls the die three times, turning up three numbers.

The object of the game is to combine any two or three of these numbers, within a given time — say, one minute — by addition, subtraction, multiplication, and division, to obtain the highest possible score.

For example, suppose a player turns up 4, 5, and 6.

He can *add* them: $4 + 5 + 6 =$	15
He can *subtract* from an addition: $(4 + 5) - 6 =$	3
He can *multiply*: $6 \times 5 =$	30
He can *divide* a multiple: $(6 \times 4) \div 4 =$	6
Total score:	54

With these same numbers a player could score even higher, with combinations like $4 + (5 \times 6) = 34$, $(5 \times 6) - 4 = 26$, $6 \times 5 \times 4 = 120$, etc.

5

ORAL GAMES

It is easier to interest a child in numbers by using an oral game introduced quite casually than by having him sit down to "do" arithmetic with paper and pencil. Hence the games in this chapter can well be used to start the "wheels of the mind" rolling in a mathematical direction.

All that most of these games require the players to do is to speak some words. So no preparation or equipment is needed except, as indicated for a few, a timer to pace the participants.

NUMBER, PLEASE

ASSOCIATION OF NUMBERS WITH FACTS AND WITH EQUIVALENCES

Two or more players

The players take turns asking each other questions requiring commonly known facts to be associated with numbers.

Here is how one such game might proceed:

Player 1: What number do you think of when I say "fingers"?

Player 2: Five, because there are five fingers on a hand. What number do you think of when I say a "quart"?

Player 3: Two, because two pints make a quart. What number do you associate with "foot"?

Player 4: Twelve, because there are twelve inches in a foot. What number do you associate with "decade"?

Player 1: What's that?

Player 4: How about you, Player 2?

Player 2: Ten, because there are ten years in a decade.

One point is scored for each correct response. A player is penalized one point for each incorrect response or for each failure to respond.

Questions can cover the whole table of equivalences (see the table in the Appendix)—days of the week, hours in a day, minutes in an hour, days in a year, months in a year, years in a century, feet in a yard, etc.

A somewhat more challenging variation requires the players to complete common phrases or titles or statements involving specific numbers. Here are a few examples:

The first *(10)* amendments to the Constitution are known as the Bill of Rights.

(13) is considered by superstitious people to be an unlucky number.

The first *(100)* years are the hardest.

A jury is composed of *(12)* good men and true.
Come *(1)*, come all!
(2)'s company; *(3)*'s a crowd.
(1), *(2)*, buckle my shoe; *(3)*, *(4)*, shut the door,
God is *(1)*.
God gave us *(10)* commandments.
Moses received from God *(2)* Tablets of the Law.
The patriots of the American Revolution had the spirit
of *('76)*.
In World War I, the soldiers went "over the top" at *(0)*
hour.
He ran like *(60)*.

The best way to play this variation is for the parent or
the leader to provide the statements and let the players
take turns trying to find the answers. Naturally, the
statements should be adapted to the players' level of
maturity. Older children might be asked to supply the
correct numbers in titles of books — *The House of the (7)
Gables, (20,000) Leagues under the Sea* — or poems like
(10) Nights in a Barroom. Or expressions may be used
such as: She was one of the *(400)* of society. Everything
was at *(6)*'s and *(7)*'s. Possession is *(9/10)* ths of the law.
The press is known as the *(4)*th estate. The *(7)* ages of
man. He arrived at the *(11)*th hour. The animals went
into the ark *(2)* by *(2)*. It's a *(100)* to *(1)* shot. A clair-
voyant has a *(6)*th sense.

BUZZ

COUNTING, MULTIPLICATION, DIVISION
Two or more players   Timer
This is a classic game — to which we have added a few
original variations — calling for alertness and concen-

tration as well as speed in the mental performance of elementary arithmetical operations.

In the simplest form of this game, the first player announces a number from 2 to 9 — say, 6 — which the participants are to avoid mentioning when they count off, each player saying one number each turn. They are also to avoid all multiples of the chosen number (for example, in this case, 12, 18, 24, etc.), as well as any number in which the original number is a digit (for example, 16, 26, etc.).

Instead of mentioning a forbidden number, a player who reaches it when his turn comes in the counting must say "Buzz." Thus, if the original forbidden number were 6, counting would proceed, player by player, as follows: 1, 2, 3, 4, 5, Buzz, 7, 8, 9, 10, 11, Buzz, 13, 14, 15, Buzz, 17, Buzz, 19, 20, 21, 22, 23, Buzz, 25, Buzz, 27, 28, 29, Buzz, 31, 32, 33, 34, 35, Buzz, 37, 38, 39, 40, 41, Buzz, 43, 44, 45, Buzz, etc.

A player scores one point if he says "Buzz" appropriately when his turn comes. He loses two points if he fails to say "Buzz" when he should or if he says it when he should not.

The game should be carried far enough for a player to score a total of ten points. The first to do so wins.

A time limit, made shorter with each round, can be set on responses in order to speed up the counting and add excitement to the game.

37

UMPTY-UM BUZZ

This variation is played just like Buzz, except that multiples of the forbidden number must be represented by as many "buzzes" as the multiplier. Thus, if the forbidden number is 7, then 14 would be "Buzz, buzz," 21 would be "Buzz, buzz, buzz," and so on.

HIPPETY-HOP BUZZ

Here the player has to hop over certain numbers by a given interval.

If the forbidden number is odd — say, 7 — and the players are required to skip one number each time they count, they would have to proceed in this way: 1, 3, 5, Buzz, 9, 11, 13, 15, Buzz, 19, Buzz, 23, 25, Buzz, etc.

As the players develop their skill, larger hops or intervals between numbers can be tried. For example, they can count by fives or sevens. The same can be done with even numbers.

MAKE IT

ADDITION, SUBTRACTION, MULTIPLICATION, DIVISION

Two or more players   Timer

"Making it" means, in this game, using any combination of two or more numbers to reach a given number from another one by addition, subtraction, multiplication, or division.

The parent or the leader begins by saying: "I have a number—5. Tell me how to make it 10." Naturally, he can choose any two numbers, but it is best to begin with small ones.

A child might answer: "Add 5, because $5 + 5 = 10$," or "Multiply by 2, because $5 \times 2 = 10$."

Similarly, a player might make 6 become 12 by multiplying 6 by 2 or by dividing 72 by 6. The number 18 could be reduced to 12 by subtracting 6 from it or dividing 18 by 3 and then multiplying the quotient (6) by 2.

A limited time should be given for each response. A player scores one point for each correct answer and is penalized one point for each error or failure to respond in time. The winner is the first to score fifteen points.

The game can be varied by requiring the players to find, within a given time limit, as many ways as possible of reaching the given number. Additional points may be awarded for each way—one point for the first, three for the second, five for the third, ten for the fourth, etc.

COIN COUNT

ADDITION, MULTIPLICATION, COIN
EQUIVALENCES

Two or more players   Timer

The object of this game is to use the fewest possible coins to total a given sum.

To begin, the parent or the leader calls out the sum to be made—for example, forty-five cents. If, within a given time limit, a player can say what coins will make this sum, he raises his hand. Different possible responses are: a quarter and two dimes; forty-five pennies; four dimes and a nickel; and nine nickels.

For each correct response, a player scores one point provided he is the first to give that response. For each incorrect response he is penalized one point. The player whose response involves the fewest number of coins that will total the required sum earns a bonus of five points.

Thus, if the sum to be made is sixty-five cents, possible responses are: a half dollar, a dime, and a nickel; sixty-five pennies; thirteen nickels; six dimes and a nickel; and two quarters, a dime, and a nickel. Each of these responses would earn one point, but the first would be worth an additional five points.

The winner is the player who first scores a total of twenty-five points.

HANDY FIGURES

ADDITION, SUBTRACTION, MULTIPLICATION, DIVISION, EQUIVALENCES

Two players only

This game calls for quick responses and places a premium on rapid mental arithmetic.

One player places his palms over the outstretched and upturned palms of the other.

The parent or the leader now calls out an equation or an equivalence involving addition, subtraction, multiplication, or division — say, $5 + 2 = 6$. This statement is, of course, false. As soon as the player with his palms underneath realizes it is false, he must try to slap the hands of his opponent before the latter pulls them away. If the first player succeeds in touching either hand of his opponent, he wins one point and gets another chance; if he fails to touch either hand of his opponent, the latter scores one point and gets his turn to put his up-turned palms underneath those of the first player.

If a true statement is made — for example, $7 \times 8 = 56$ — neither player must move his hands. If either one does, whether by trying to slap his opponent's hands or by withdrawing his hands, his opponent scores one point and wins a turn to have his palms underneath.

Statements can include such equivalences as: 4 quarts = 1 gallon; 12 inches = 1 foot; etc.

The first to score twenty-five points is the winner.

SNATCH MATCH

ADDITION, SUBTRACTION, MULTIPLICATION, DIVISION, EQUIVALENCES

Two players only   Checker or bottle cap

This is a variation of Handy Figures, above, that also calls for rapid responses, both mental and physical.

Place on the table any small object, like a checker or a bottle cap. The two players stand on opposite sides of the table, equally distant from the object, but within easy reach of it.

The parent or the leader now makes a statement involving arithmetic or equivalences. The statement may be true or false. If the statement is true, each player must attempt to snatch the object from the table before his opponent does. The one who gets the object scores one point. If the statement is false, the object must remain on the table untouched. If either player touches the object, he is penalized one point, and his opponent scores a point.

The first player to score fifteen points wins.

SNATCH-A-BATCH

ADDITION, SUBTRACTION, MULTIPLICATION, DIVISION, EQUIVALENCES

Two players only   Checkers or bottle caps

After you have played a few rounds of Snatch Match, above, you might like to try this more challenging variation.

Instead of one checker or bottle cap, place ten on the table.

Again the players are positioned at opposite ends of the table, and the teacher or the leader makes statements, true or false, that involve arithmetic or equivalences.

If a statement is true, no one is to make a move. Anyone touching the objects in that case is penalized three points, and his opponent scores one point.

But if a statement is false, the first one to snatch the exact number of objects that corrects the statement scores five points. Anyone who snatches the wrong number is penalized three points. The winner is the first to score thirty points.

For example, suppose the caller says: "5 + 1 = 8." Since the statement is false, and since 5 + 1 + 2 = 8, the first player to snatch two checkers or bottle caps scores five points.

On the other hand, if the caller says: "6 + 1 = 7" or "There are seven days in a week," anyone who snatches anything loses three points, and his opponent scores one point.

Of course, the game can be made more complicated by adding to the number of objects on the table and making statements that combine two or more arithmetical operations, like addition and division, or subtraction and multiplication.

WHAT'S THE DIFFERENCE?

COUNTING BY TWOS, THREES, FOURS, ETC.

Two or more players   Timer

The first player begins by calling out any three successive numbers in a series in which the difference between every number and its successor is 2. For example, he may start with 5, 7, 9.

The next player must, within a given time limit, continue the same series from where the preceding player left off, carrying it along for three more numbers—in this case, 11, 13, 15.

The other players, in turn, follow the same procedure—17, 19, 21; 23, 25, 27; 29, 31, 33; etc., until one player makes a mistake. The player who gives a wrong response is penalized one point.

Now a new series is begun, this time with a difference of three between successive numbers—for example, 18, 21, 24; 27, 30, 33; 36, 39, 42; etc. Each time an error is made, the player who makes it is penalized one point, and a new series is begun, so that the players may be counting by fours, fives, sixes, sevens, and so on.

A player with three points against him is out of the game. The winner is the survivor after all his competitors have been eliminated.

FINGER FIGURES

ADDITION, SUBTRACTION

Two players only

Did you know that the word "digit" comes from a Latin word meaning "finger"? That should not be surprising, because it is natural for all of us to count on our fingers. So our ten fingers may truly be said to be the first "digital computers"!

In this game, when the first player says, "One, two, three, finger shoot!" both players extend one or more fingers of one hand. The first player then adds the total number of fingers extended. He next subtracts the smaller number from the larger. He adds the remainder to the first sum to get his score.

For example, if one player extends three fingers and the other extends four, $3 + 4 = 7$ and $4 - 3 = 1$: $1 + 7 = 8$. In this case, eight would be the first player's score.

It is now the second player's turn to say, "One, two, three, finger shoot!" If he extends five fingers and his opponent extends three, then the second player's score is calculated in this fashion: $5 + 3 = 8$ and $5 - 3 = 2$: $8 + 2 = 10$.

If both players extend three fingers, then the score would be calculated thus: $3 + 3 = 6$ and $3 - 3 = 0$: $6 +$ bonus of 10 (because both players extended the same number of fingers) $= 16$.

To win, a player must score fifty points.

DIGITAL COMPUTER

MULTIPLICATION, DIVISION

Two players only

In this variation of Finger Figures, the procedure is the same except that the score of each player is determined by adding the product of the two numbers to their quotient, rounded off, if necessary, to a whole number.

For example, if one player extends four fingers, and the other extends three, the score is calculated in this way: $4 \times 3 = 12$ and $4 \div 3 = 1$ (rounded off): $12 + 1 = 13$.

A bonus of 10 points is scored if both players extend the same number of fingers. The winner is the first player to score 200 points.

FINGER SHOOT

ADDITION, SUBTRACTION, MULTIPLICATION, DIVISION

Two players only

In this variation, the players "shoot" at the target number called by the one who says, "One, two, three, finger shoot!" Suppose, for example, that the target number is 2. If one player extends five fingers, and the other extends 3, the target can be reached by subtracting 3 from 5.

Five points are scored for hitting the target. If the target is missed, nothing is scored. The winner is the first player to score twenty-five points.

GAZINTAS

DIVISION, MULTIPLICATION

Two players   Timer

The name of this game is derived from what you sound like when you say "goes into" very fast, as in the expression, "6 gazinta 18 three times."

Each of the players, in turn, gives his opponent clues that are divisors of larger numbers that the opponent must find within a given time limit.

For example, a player may say, "3 goes into my number, but 4 does not." The numbers chosen may be from 1 to 100. Young children may be given a clue as to the size of the number—for instance, "My number is less than 25."

Suppose that, with these clues, the other player guesses that the number is 6. This is divisible by 3, but not by 4. However, he may be told that this is not the number meant. In that case, he will have to be given another clue. The first player may add, "5 goes into my number, but 6 does not."

In that case, the number must be 15, which is divisible by 3 and 5, but not by 4 and 6. If the second player hits on the right number within the time limit, the first player gets two points because two guesses and two sets of clues were needed to reach the right answer. Naturally, a player tries to get the right number with as few clues as possible, and his opponent tries to pick a number that will require as many clues as possible.

The game continues in this way until one player attains a score of twenty points. He is the winner.

6

PAPER-AND-PENCIL GAMES

After you have captured your child's interest with a few oral games, it should not be difficult to involve him in playing with paper and pencil. Using written figures aids his mental arithmetic and fixes its results. At the same time, he can learn numerical notation, both Arabic and Roman, as well as the conventional signs for addition, subtraction, multiplication, division, fractions, decimals, coordinates, and so forth.

NUMBER MAZE

COUNTING; ODD, EVEN, PRIME, AND
COMPOSITE NUMBERS
Two, three, or four players
The first player writes the number 1 anywhere on a large sheet of blank paper and places a dot next to it.

The second player writes a 2 anywhere else on the paper and places a dot next to it. The players continue in this fashion until they reach the number 20.

Now the first player connects the dot next to the number 1 with the dot next to the number 2, using either a straight or a curved line. The next player does the same, carrying the line to the dot next to the number 3, but without touching or crossing the first line. The players proceed in this way, continuing the line from one number to the next higher number, but without ever touching or crossing any line.

If a player touches or crosses any line, he is penalized one point. If he crosses the intersection of two or more lines, he is penalized two points. And if he draws a line to the wrong dot, he is penalized three points. He scores one point for doing the right thing. The player with the highest score after five rounds is the winner.

The game may be varied by having the players first connect the odd numbers—1, 3, 5, 7, etc.—up to 19 and then proceed to the even numbers—2, 4, 6, 8—up to 20. In still other rounds, the first player can connect the first prime number (2) with the next (3), and the other players would proceed from there to 5 and the other prime numbers until the last prime number was reached (19). They would then go on to the first composite number (4) to the next (6) and up to 20.

Finally, the difficulty of the game can be escalated by using larger numbers: 20 to 40, 40 to 60, etc.

ARITHME-TIC-TAC-TOE

ADDITION, SUBTRACTION
Two players only
This is a simple adaptation of an old game.

First introduce the child to tic-tac-toe if he does not already know it. Draw the pattern of two horizontal lines crossing two vertical lines, as shown. The two players take turns marking squares, one player using Xs and the other 0s. The winner is the first to mark a row of three in any direction—vertically, horizontally, or diagonally.

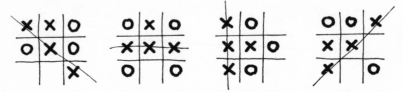

We are now ready for the arithmetical counterpart of tic-tac-toe. The same pattern is used, but this time each player enters, in turn, the numbers 1, 2, and 3, *in that order,* in place of an X or an 0. (To distinguish between the numbers inserted by each player, one may use a red pencil and the other a blue, or one of the players may underline or circle his numbers, as shown.)

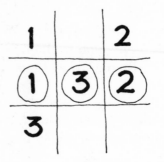

The winner of the round is the player who succeeds in placing his numbers in a row of three in any direction. As $1 + 2 + 3 = 6$, the winner here scores six points.

With each round, the players alternate going first. The first player to score twenty-four points wins.

Of course, when the players are evenly matched, a stalemate is also possible, like the one shown here.

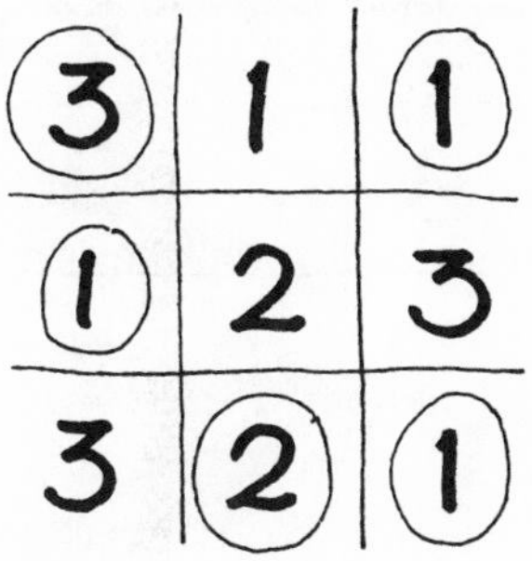

CRISSCROSS

ADDITION, SUBTRACTION, ODD AND EVEN NUMBERS

Two players only

This variation of Arithme-Tic-Tac-Toe, is played in a similar way except that one player uses only odd numbers (1, 3, 5, 7, 9), while his opponent uses only even numbers (0, 2, 4, 6, 8). No number may be used more than once. The players take turns inserting their numbers into the boxes until one player wins the round by making a sum of fifteen in any direction.

In the game illustrated, the player with the odd numbers went first. He began with the 7. The second player inserted the 8. The third move was the insertion of the 5. Since $5 + 7 = 12$, and $15 - 12 = 3$, an odd number, the second player, in order to prevent his opponent from winning, inserted the 2 in the vertical row between the 5 and the 7.

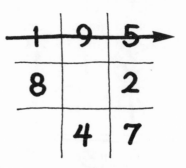

Next, the first player inserted the 9. At this point the second player was in a dilemma. If, in order to prevent his opponent from putting a 1 into the first horizontal box and winning the game ($1 + 9 + 5 = 15$), the second player had put any even number remaining to him (4 or 6) into that box, he would have made it possible for the first player to win by completing the first vertical row with the insertion of an odd number still remaining to him (3 or 1), because $4 + 8 + 3 = 6 + 8 + 1 = 15$. But by placing his 4 where he did, the second player left the first horizontal box to his opponent, who won the game by putting a 1 there.

The winner of each round scores fifteen. The players take turns going first until one scores a total of sixty points.

NUMBER ROW

ADDITION, SUBTRACTION

Two players only

In this variation, the same procedure is followed as in Crisscross, above, but each player may use, just once, *any* digit, odd or even, from 0 to 9. The players can distinguish their respective numbers with different colors or by underlining or circling them, as illustrated below. The object is to make a sum of fifteen in any direction. Scoring is the same.

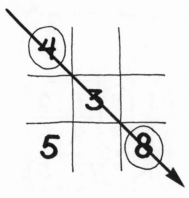

CONFIGURATIONS

ADDITION, SUBTRACTION, MULTIPLICATION

Two or more players

Each player first makes for himself a square of sixteen boxes and enters at random the digits from 1 through 9, repeating some of them as desired.

In the simplest form of this game, the parent or the teacher begins by calling out any number from 3 through

18. Each player then checks his pattern to see whether he has two numbers, arranged vertically, horizontally, or diagonally, that add up to the given number. The player who sees these configurations draws a line surrounding the two numbers and shows them to everyone else, as a check on his arithmetic. Once a number has been thus enclosed, it cannot be used again to form another sum.

For example, in the pattern illustrated below, if the number 12 had been called out, there are three combinations that add up to it: 9 + 3 diagonally, 8 + 4 vertically, and 7 + 5 horizontally. These six numbers have been enclosed in loops.

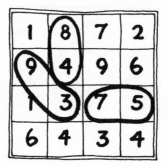

The game continues in this way, as different numbers are called for, until one player has enclosed all the figures in one row, one column, or one diagonal.

After a few rounds of addition, the game can be played to provide practice in subtraction. In that case, the numbers called for should be from 0 through 8. A series of rounds involving multiplication can also be played if the numbers called for range from 2 through 81.

To add to the difficulty, increase the number of boxes in the square to twenty-five and raise correspondingly the figures inserted in the boxes and the numbers called for. Further complications can be obtained by requiring three, instead of two, numbers to form a winning configuration.

PRODUCT NET

MULTIPLICATION, DIVISION, FACTORING

Two or more players

Each player makes a square of sixteen boxes. At the top of each vertical column and to the left of each horizontal row he then enters at random the numbers from 2 through 9, as illustrated here.

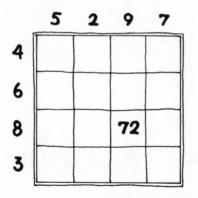

The first player begins by calling out a number that is the product of any number to the left of a horizontal row on his square and a number at the top of a vertical column. For example, using the square shown here, he might call out the number 72. At the same time, he writes this number in the box where the column headed by 9 intersects with the row with 8 at its left.

Each of the players now checks his own square to see whether he too can find a box in a row with one factor of 72 at its side and in a column headed by another factor of the same number. If he can, he inserts 72 in the appropriate box, as shown.

The players take turns calling out numbers, and the game continues in this fashion until one player has inserted products in four boxes horizontally, vertically, or diagonally. As the winner of the round, he scores five points. Additional rounds should be played, with different number patterns. The player with the highest score after five rounds wins the game.

With experience, players can prepare their squares so that they can make two entries at the same time. For example, $4 \times 3 = 12$ and $6 \times 2 = 12$. To achieve this, the 4 and the 6 would have to be placed at the head of different columns, and the 3 and the 2 at the left of different rows, or vice versa.

SQUARE ACCOUNTS

ADDITION, SUBTRACTION

Two or more players

Each player first prepares a square consisting of sixteen boxes. To the right of each of the four horizontal rows and beneath each of the four vertical rows he then writes a different number ranging from 15 through 25, or eight numbers in all, as illustrated here. The numbers may be in any order, but no number may be repeated.

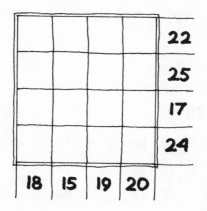

Next, every player, in turn, calls out a number from 1 through 9, and he as well as every other player enters that number in any box in his square. These numbers may be repeated.

When all the boxes have been filled in, each player adds the numbers in the boxes in each of the four horizontal rows in his square and enters the total, in each case, in the space to the left of the row. He also adds the numbers in each of the four vertical columns and places the sum in the space above the column.

If the sum written above a column equals the number written beneath the same column, or if the sum written to the left of a horizontal row equals the number written to the right of that row, a player scores five points. If the sums differ by one, he scores four points. If they differ by two, he scores three points. If they differ by three, he scores two points. If they differ by four, he scores one point. And if they differ by five or more, he scores zero for that particular column or row.

Following these rules, let us, for example, calculate the respective scores of two players having the squares shown below.

Player **A**

	15	29	20	25	
21	4	4	7	6	16
28	7	10	1	10	20
23	3	9	4	7	22
17	1	6	8	2	18
	17	15	19	21	

Player **B**

	16	26	24	23	
19	4	10	4	1	18
19	2	6	4	7	20
33	9	7	10	7	19
18	1	3	6	8	16
	15	22	21	25	

Starting from the first (extreme left) column of player A's square, we find:

$17 - 15 = 2$ Score 3 points
$29 - 15 = 14$ Score 0 points
$20 - 19 = 1$ Score 4 points
$25 - 21 = 4$ Score 1 point
                Total 8 points for the columns.

Starting from the top horizontal row of the same square, we find:

$21 - 16 = 5$ Score 0 points
$28 - 20 = 8$ Score 0 points
$23 - 22 = 1$ Score 4 points
$18 - 17 = 1$ Score 4 points
                Total 8 points for the rows.

This makes $8 + 8 = 16$ points in all for player A.

Using the same procedure in scoring player B's square, we obtain:

$16 - 15 = 1$	Score 4 points
$26 - 22 = 4$	Score 1 point
$24 - 21 = 3$	Score 2 points
$25 - 23 = 2$	Score <u>3</u> points
	Total 10 points for the columns.

$19 - 18 = 1$	Score 4 points
$20 - 19 = 1$	Score 4 points
$33 - 19 = 14$	Score 0 points
$18 - 16 = 2$	Score <u>3</u> points
	Total 11 points for the rows.

This makes $11 + 10 = 21$ points in all for Player B.

In successive rounds, each player should begin with a new square having a different pattern of numbers to the right of the rows and beneath the columns.

The player with the highest score after five rounds is the winner of the game.

IMPRISONED NUMBERS

ADDITION, SUBTRACTION, MULTIPLICATION
Two players only
Draw a sixteen-box square with four boxes on each side. Write in the boxes, at random, the numbers from 1 to

16. In any two boxes insert an X before the number, and in any three other boxes make the number negative by preceding it with a minus sign (−).

The first player darkens and thickens any one of the four lines surrounding any number. His opponent does the same. They take turns doing this until one box has three of its sides darkened and thickened. The player whose turn it is next *must* now darken and thicken the fourth side of this box, thereby capturing and imprisoning the number in it.

Capturing a number in this way and imprisoning it may be to a player's advantage or disadvantage, depending on the number and its value. A player scores the value of any number he imprisons if it does not have an X or a minus sign in front of it. If he is lucky and imprisons a number with an X in front of it, he first adds this number to his accumulated score and then doubles the amount. For example, if a player has accumulated 20 points and imprisons a 4 with an X in front of it, he first adds the 4 to 20 to make 24 and then doubles the sum to make 48. But if the captured and imprisoned number has a minus sign in front of it, its value must be subtracted from the player's accumulated score. Thus, if a player has scored 18 and imprisons −9, his score falls to 9.

The game is continued in this way until all the numbers have been captured and imprisoned. As a player imprisons a number, he initials the box containing it or checks it with a colored pencil—one player red, and the other player blue.

The one with the higher total score wins the game.

7

CARD GAMES

Children love to play cards. Why not, therefore, use cards as aids in teaching arithmetic? After all, the cards already have numbers on them, and parents and teachers have found that youngsters willingly and rapidly learn to perform basic arithmetical operations when these form part of a familiar or intriguing card game. For example, rummy, casino, and pinochle offer the child practice in forming mathematical sets, and such well-known games as casino and twenty-one involve much addition. Here, then, are some new as well as some old games with playing cards that combine fun with practice in arithmetic.

SOME SUMS!

ADDITION
One player only

For this game of solitaire, the picture cards—king, queen, and jack—count as 10 each.

After shuffling the deck, the player first places four cards faceup side by side on the table, as shown here.

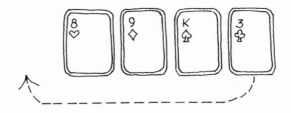

Now, he may rearrange these four cards by moving any one in an effort to place side by side three cards that add up to 10, 20, or 30. For example, with the four cards shown here, the player can shift the 3 at the right around to the left end to line up with the 8 and the 9, making a row of three cards that add up to 20.

After removing these three cards to a separate pile, the player replaces them with three additional cards drawn from the top of the deck and repeats the procedure. If, no matter how he arranges the four cards, he cannot get three adjacent cards to add up to 10, 20, or 30, he draws from the deck and lays down, one by one, additional cards and keeps trying.

The game ends when the player has drawn all the cards from the deck. If no cards are left on the table—that is, if all the cards have been removed—the player has a perfect score. Otherwise, he counts the cards remaining on the table to determine his score. He can then try another round, after shuffling the pack, to see whether he can score lower.

SUM BUILDING

ADDITION

Two players only

This is an adaptation of Some Sums! for two players. Once again, the picture cards count 10 each.

After the cards have been shuffled, each player is dealt three. Then the first player draws one card from the turned-down deck and tries to find in his hand three that add up to 10, 20, or 30. If he does so, he lays these three cards faceup on the table near him and is credited with their sum. He thus gets a chance to draw three more cards from the top of the deck and to try again. If he cannot find such a combination in his hand, he discards one card, laying it faceup on the table.

His opponent can then pick up the discarded card (top card of discard pile only) if he can use it to make a scoring combination, or he can take one from the deck.

The game proceeds in this way until all the cards have been used. Winner of the round is the player with the higher score.

PYRAMID

ADDITION

One player only

This is an easy game of solitaire.

The player arranges twenty-eight playing cards faceup in the form of a pyramid, as shown here, with seven horizontal rows, each overlapping the one above it. The first row consists of seven cards, the second of six, and so on, to the apex of the pyramid, which consists of one card. The rest of the deck is held in the player's hand, facedown.

In this game, the king counts 13; the queen, 12; and the jack, 11.

The player begins by removing from the bottom row of seven any two cards that total thirteen (or a king, if there is one). These cards are set aside in a separate pile. If the two cards that have been removed thereby uncover completely a card in the row above, it may be used, in combination with another card in the bottom row, to make a total of thirteen. The cards removed at any time—whether a king alone or two cards totaling thirteen—must always be free, that is, completely uncovered, with no card or cards overlapping.

If the player cannot find free cards adding up to thirteen, he turns up the top card in the pack in his hand. He may use this to combine with any free card in the pyramid to total thirteen and remove both cards to the pile of thirteens. If he cannot use the top card in this way, he must lay it faceup on the table and begin a stockpile. He may use the top card of this pile at any time to make a combination totaling thirteen. He then proceeds to turn up the next top card in his hand and continues in this way until all the cards in his hand have been turned up, whether used to make combinations of thirteen or placed in the stockpile.

If the player has not removed all the cards in the pyramid, he may turn the stockpile over and go through it one card at a time as he did with the original pack. The whole stockpile may be turned over three times, but it must not be shuffled. If all the cards in the pyramid have not been removed after the stockpile has been turned over three times, the game is lost. Yet it is often possible to win without turning the stockpile over even once.

After a few rounds, the player can raise the sum to be reached to fifteen and follow the same procedure. A still more challenging form of the same game involves using two or three cards to make a total of twenty or twenty-one.

SAM PYRAMID

SUBTRACTION, ADDITION, MULTIPLICATION
One player only
SAM is our abbreviation for Subtraction, Addition, and Multiplication.

This variation is played just like Pyramid, but the player uses two or three cards and SAM to attain a figure of twenty. Any two of these three operations may be used at one time—multiplication and addition, multiplication and subtraction, addition and subtraction, addition and addition, subtraction and subtraction, etc.

Suppose, for example, that the player had uncovered a king, a 3, and a 4. These three add up to 20. A 4 and a 5, multiplied, also make 20. A queen, a 3, and a 5 likewise add up to 20. A jack, a 1, and a 10 can be arranged thus: $(11 - 1) + 10 = 20$. Many other possible combinations will occur to the player as he ponders his problem.

MADS PYRAMID

MULTIPLICATION, ADDITION, DIVISION, SUBTRACTION
One or two players
This can be played as a game of solitaire, like Pyramid, or two players can take turns trying to clear the pyramid. In that case, a record should be kept of the cards removed by each player. The winner is the player who removes the greater number of cards. An extra bonus of five points goes to the one who clears the pyramid.

In this variation the player or players use two, three, or four cards to attain the figure of twenty. But they may use MADS—that is, any combination of Multiplication, Addition, Division, and Subtraction that will attain the desired result. For example, if a player uncovers a queen, a 3, and a 5, he may remove them by means of the following operation: $(12 \div 3) \times 5 = 20$. A player with 12, 4, 7, and 1 can perform the following calculation: $[(12 \div 4) \times 7] - 1 = (3 \times 7) - 1 = 20$.

Players must do the calculations aloud so that their opponent may check and challenge if necessary.

TIC-TAC BINGO

ADDITION, MULTIPLICATION
Two players only
Shuffle the cards and lay them out facedown as shown.

The first player turns up a card; then the second player turns up a card. This continues until one player has turned up three cards that are the same color (all red or all black) and that lie in a row (horizontal, vertical, or diagonal).

To compute the score, take the sum of the value of the cards in the winning row. An extra bonus is awarded if all the cards in the winning row are of the same suit. When this occurs, double the score value. For example, if the winning row consists of heart 6, heart 9, and heart 3, the score is 18 and the bonus doubles it, making a final score of 36.

Several rounds should be played until one player wins by scoring at least 300 points.

WAR

COUNTING, DISTINGUISHING BETWEEN
GREATER AND LESS

Two, three, or four players

Divide the deck evenly among the players, dealing one card at a time. If there are three players, remove one card from the deck, so that the remaining fifty-one cards can be distributed equally among them.

Each player stacks his cards facedown in front of him.

The first player draws a card from the top of his deck and places it faceup on the table. The next player does the same. The one whose card has the higher numerical value takes both cards and places them facedown at the bottom of his stack. If neither card is higher – say, both are 5s – the battle is drawn. Both cards are left on the table faceup. Each player now puts another card faceup over the first one, and the higher card now takes in all four cards.

If the second set of two cards also match, the war continues until one player lays down a card with a higher numerical value than his opponent and takes all the cards lying faceup.

Sooner or later one player will have lost all the cards in his stack, and another will have won the war.

MADS WAR

MULTIPLICATION, ADDITION, DIVISION, SUBTRACTION

Two players

In this variation of War, the players use MADS – that is, Multiplication, Addition, Division, and Subtraction – on the numerical values of the cards they draw, in an effort to make a match.

After the cards have been thoroughly shuffled and laid facedown on the table, each player, in turn, draws two from the top of the deck, one at a time, and lays them faceup in front of him.

Let us say that the first player has drawn a 5 and a 1; and the second player, an 8 and a 3.

Now the first player attacks with MADS, thus: M: $5 \times 1 =$ 5. A: $5 + 1 = 6$. D: $5 \div 1 = 5$. S: $5 - 1 = 4$.

Performing the same operations on his cards, the second player gets these results: M: $8 \times 3 = 24$. A: $8 + 3 = 11$. D: $8 \div 3 = 2 \, 2/3 = 3$ (rounded off to the nearest whole number). S: $8 - 3 = 5$.

Since the first player's two 5s match the 5 of the second player, the first player picks up all the cards.

In the second round, his opponent attacks. If he can make a match with MADS, he collects the cards. If not, the cards remain on the table, and the winner of the next round picks them up. If there is no winner in the next round, the cards remain on the table until, in some subsequent round, they are picked up by the winner.

The game ends when all the cards have been used up. At that point, each player counts his cards and receives one point for each. However, if at any time the two cards turned up together are of the same color, a player with such a pair scores a bonus of five points. In fact, any set of two—two 4s or two 5s, for example—turned up together adds five points to the player's score.

The player with the higher score wins the game.

FRACTION WAR

FRACTIONS, DISTINGUISHING BETWEEN
GREATER AND LESS
Two, three, or four players
Remove all the picture cards from the deck.

Shuffle and deal four cards to each player, one card at a time. Place the rest of the pack facedown on the table.

The first player selects two cards from his hand: one, red; and one, black. If he does not have one card of each color in his hand, he may draw two cards at a time from the pack on the table. He now forms a fraction with the numerical value of the red card as the numerator and with that of the black card as the denominator. Thus, a red 5 and a black 6 become 5/6.

The next player follows the same procedure. Let us say his fraction is 4/3. Comparing 4/3 with 5/6, he declares 4/3 to be the higher and collects both sets of cards, placing them facedown in a pile next to him. He then sets out another fraction, drawing two cards at a time, if necessary, from the pack ᴜɴ the table. If the fractions of both players are equal, the battle is drawn, and both sets of cards remain faceup. The player who wins the next time collects all the cards.

The game continues until all the cards from the table pack have been used and one player cannot place any cards on the table to form a fraction. Each player scores one point for each card he has collected. Several rounds should be played until one player scores fifty points. He is the winner.

FRACTION BLACKJACK

ADDITION AND SUBTRACTION OF FRACTIONS,
DISTINGUISHING BETWEEN GREATER
AND LESS

Two or more players

In this game, all the picture cards are wild and may be given any value from 1 to 10.

The cards should be separated into two packs, one consisting of hearts and diamonds (red cards) and the other of clubs and spades (black cards). The two packs should be laid facedown on the table.

The first player draws one card from each pack and forms a fraction by using the numerical value of the black card as the numerator and the value of the red card as the denominator. Thus, if he draws black 5 and red 4, his fraction is $5/4 = 1\ 1/4$. The same player continues, drawing two more cards, one black and the other red, and again forms a fraction, whose value he adds to the previous one. For example, if he draws black jack and red 5, and if he gives the jack a value of 10, his fraction becomes $10/5 = 2$, and the sum of his two fractions is $1\ 1/4 + 2 = 3\ 1/4$. He continues in this way until he makes a sum of 10 or gets as close to 10, either above or below it, as he can.

Each player in turn does the same, trying to equal or beat his opponents in the closeness to which he comes to a sum of 10. The game ends when all the cards from the two packs have been used up. The winner is the player who comes closest to a sum of 10.

In other rounds other targets may be substituted for 10 – for example, 5 or 6.

FLIP-COUNT

COUNTING, ADDITION, SUBTRACTION
Two or more players
Shuffle a deck of cards and place it facedown on the table.

The first player begins the count with 1 and at the same time flips the top card faceup. He scores the value of the card minus 1. Thus if he flips up a king, he scores $13 - 1 = 12$; if a queen, $12 - 1 = 11$; if a jack, $11 - 1 = 10$; and so on.

The next player now continues the count with 2 and flips up the next card. His score is calculated by subtracting 2 from the value of the card he flipped up. So, for example, $2 - 2 = 0$.

As the count goes higher with each player, his score is determined by subtracting the lower number from the higher, whether the number reached in the count or the value of the card. Thus, if the fourth player turns up a 2, he subtracts this from his count of 4, to get a score of 2.

The game continues until all the cards in the deck have been flipped up. Each player then adds the points he has scored. The one with the lowest number wins the game.

GIVE AND TAKE

ADDITION, SUBTRACTION

Two, three, or four players

In this game too, the king counts for 13; the queen, for 12; and the jack, for 11.

After shuffling the cards thoroughly, the dealer gives each player three, one at a time, proceeding from left to right.

The object of the game is to produce a given sum by adding the numerical values of the cards in one's hand.

Suppose, for example, that the target sum agreed upon is 21, and the first player has in his hand 8, 9, and 6. This add up to 23, a little too much. In that case, he may say, "I'll trade a 9 for a number less than 8," in the hope of getting a 7 and thus reaching 21: $6 + 8 + 7 = 21$. Of course, he does not specify the exact number he is looking for. He just says, ". . . a number less than 8," or ". . . a number greater than 6."

Now all the players look at their hands and decide whether such a trade would be of advantage to them. Naturally, in the process they are adding and subtracting mentally, and any mistakes they make could cost them the opportunity of scoring. If no one is willing to trade, the next player takes his turn.

Suppose that the second player has a hand with 10, 6, and 12 (queen). He may decide to trade his queen for a card less than 6, in the hope of getting a 5 and thus hitting the target: $10 + 6 + 5 = 21$.

The game proceeds in this way until one player succeeds in getting a hand that adds up to the target number. He scores three points.

After each player has had his chance, the cards in their hands are laid faceup on the table. The player whose hand comes closest to adding up to the target number scores one point. Thus, in this particular game, if one player's hand adds up to 23, another's to 18, a third player's to 24, and a fourth's to 20, the fourth player gets credit for one point. If two players are tied, each gets one point.

The game continues, with other deals and other targets — say, 24, 25, 31, etc. — until one player has scored ten points. He is the winner.

TABLE NUMBERS

MULTIPLICATION, DIVISION
Two or more players
The "table" in this game is the multiplication table.

After removing the four kings from the deck, shuffle the cards and lay the deck facedown within reach of the players.

The parent or the teacher now calls out a number from 1 to 12 — say, 6. He will then say, "We are looking for other numbers in the 6 table." This means that the players are to aim at producing multiples of 6 — 6, 12, 18, etc.—by multiplying the numerical values of the cards they draw.

If, for example, the first player draws from the top of the deck a 4 and an 8, he first multiplies them to see what their product is—in this case, it is 32—and then decides whether this product is a multiple of the given number, 6. A correct response here would be: "No, 32 is not a number in the 6 table."

The game continues in this way, with each player taking his turn to draw two cards, until all the cards have been drawn.

A player scores one point for any correct response, even though the number that is the product of the numerical values of the cards he has drawn is not in the given table. If it is, however, and the player sees this, he scores two points. If the cards drawn are of the same color—both red or both black—his score is doubled. For example, the queen of spades, and the 3 of clubs have 36 as their product, which is in the 6 table. Therefore, the player would score two points for recognizing this fact and would multiply this score by two, for a total score of four, because the cards were of the same color.

The score is multiplied by four if both cards drawn belong to the same suit—two diamonds, two spades, two hearts, or two clubs.

Several rounds should be played, each time with a different table—for example, with multiples of 5, 8, etc.

The winner of the game is the first player to attain a score of twenty-five points.

ADD-JOINING CARDS

ADDITION, MULTIPLICATION

Solitaire, or two, three, or four players

First, let us see how a child might play this game all by himself.

Remove the four kings from the deck, leaving forty-eight cards. Let the jack count for 11, and the queen for 12.

After shuffling the pack thoroughly, deal the cards, faceup, in a column, one under the other. If two adjacent — or, we might say, "add-joining" — cards add up to seven or to any multiple of seven, remove them.

The object of the game is to remove all the cards. If any cards remain, the number of cards left on the table represents the score. Naturally, the higher the score, the poorer the performance of the player.

If a player does not win the first time, let him try again to see whether he can better his score.

When cards are removed, the cards left "add-joining" can be added to see whether they sum up to seven or to any multiple of it. For example, in a sequence like 9, 3, and 4, if the 3 and the 4 are removed, the 9 can be then added to the "add-joining" card. If the next two cards are 7 and 5, all three cards can be removed, because $9 + 7 + 5 = 21$, a multiple of seven.

If a joker is added to the collection, it can be given any desired numerical value.

The same procedure can be used with different numbers as the target—for example, six and all multiples of it.

If two, three, or four play the game, the size of the deck can be adjusted accordingly. In that case, the dealer lays out the cards in as many columns as there are players. Thus, if there are three in the game, the table might look like this:

Player A	Player B	Player C
5	9	6
10	5	4
6	8	5
2	1	queen

With seven as the target, Player A can remove the first three cards, which total 21; Player B can remove the first two, which total 14; and Player C can remove the 4, 5, and queen, which likewise total 21.

One point is scored for each card removed. The player with the higher or highest score wins.

Again, jokers can be introduced to be used for any desired numerical values, and other numbers, like eight or ten, can be made the targets.

29 GAME

ADDITION
Two, three, or four players
In this game, each picture card—jack, queen, and king—counts as 1, as does the ace.

After being shuffled thoroughly, the cards are dealt two at a time to each player, facedown, from left to right, until the entire deck is dealt out. For this purpose, it may be necessary to adjust the size of the deck according to the number of players.

Each player picks up his cards and holds them in the shape of a fan.

Let us follow a typical game with four players.

The first player lays down a card from his hand, faceup on the table. Suppose it is a 10.

Now the second player will put one of his cards on top of the 10 — say, an 8. He then announces the total thus far: $10 + 8 = 18$.

The object of the game is to make the sum of 29 exactly — no more and no less.

If the third player lays down a 6, he says, "$18 + 6 = 24$."

Now if the fourth player can add a 5 from his hand, he can say, "$24 + 5 = 29$," and collect all the cards. In that case, he places another card from his hand faceup on the table — say, a 9.

The first player may add a king, which is equal to 1, saying, "$9 + 1 = 10$."

If the second player adds a 3, making the sum 13, and the third player puts down a queen, totaling 14, and the fourth player lays down a 5, to raise the amount to 19, the first player may collect all the cards on the table if he can add a 10. He then starts the round again — say, with an 8. An additional 7 makes the sum 15; a jack adds 1 to total 16; a queen adds another 1 to make 17; and another 7 brings the sum to 24. Then the player whose turn comes next can collect all the cards and win the trick with a 5.

If a player cannot lay down a card without making the sum go over 29, the game ends at this point, and the one with the greatest number of cards collected wins. After eight tricks have been played, the game stops, and all the collected cards are counted. The player with the greatest number wins.

When only three players participate, remove from the deck one 10 and one 9, and make the goal of a trick 10 instead of 29.

TARGET 31

ADDITION, SUBTRACTION, MULTIPLICATION, DIVISION
Two or more players
For this game, use just the 1 through 6 of each suit.

After shuffling the cards, place them facedown on the table.

Each player in succession turns up a card from the top of the deck. He adds its numerical value to the total value of all the cards turned up by preceding players. The target aimed at is precisely the sum of 31.

Thus the first player may turn up a 6; the second, a 5, making a total of 11; the third, a 3, totaling 14; the first, another 6, adding up to 20; the second, another 5, making 25; and the third, a 4, reaching the sum of 29. Now, if the first player should turn up still another 6, he must pass, because the total, 35, is greater than 31. He puts the 6 in a discard pile. Similarly, if the second player turns up a 3, he too must pass, because the new total (based on 29, the last total below 31) is 32, still too large. He therefore places his 3 in the discard pile. However, if the third player turns up a 2, he picks up all the cards making the total of 31 and receives one point for each. He is the winner of the round, with a score, in this case, of 7.

Play five rounds to see which player can score the most, or make the goal of the game a score of 25 points. If more cards are needed to continue the game, the discarded cards of players who have passed should be turned over and used again.

The target can be raised gradually to 38, 45, 52, etc.

The game may be varied by assigning different arithmetical operations to different suits. For example, if clubs involve multiplication by two, then a 3 of clubs would equal 6. Diamonds can be made to add three to the numerical value of a card. In that case, a 5 of diamonds would be equivalent to 8. Hearts could require division by two, so that a 6 of hearts would amount to only 3. And spades could penalize the player with a loss of one, making a 4 of spades equivalent to just 3. Of course, other operational values can be given to the respective suits in different rounds.

MULTISUM

ADDITION, MULTIPLICATION, DIVISION

Two players only

In this game, the jack counts for 11; the queen, for 12; and the king, for 13.

Shuffle the cards and place them facedown on the table.

Decide on a target number between 2 and 9. Let us, for example, begin with a low number – say, 3.

The first player now turns up a card from the top of the deck – say, a 7 – and lays it faceup on the table.

His opponent then draws a card – say, an 8. Since the sum of 7 and 8 is 15, a multiple of 3, the second player performs the calculation and removes the two cards to his pile. This earns him another chance to draw a card. If he now draws a 9, which is also a multiple of 3, he may remove that card, too, and add it to his pile and draw again.

Let us follow the game from this point.

Second player: 7.
First player: king = 13.
Second player: 2.

If the second player lays the 2 down on the table and removes his hand from it without picking it up with the king (king + 2 = 15), his opponent, on seeing that they add up to a multiple of 3, may claim the two cards for his pile. On the other hand, if a player makes a claim that is found to be incorrect, he must give his opponent three cards.

When the players have gone through the entire deck in this way, each counts the number of cards he has collected in his pile. The player with the greater number of cards scores ten points.

Then the players add the numerical values of the cards in their respective piles. The one with the higher sum receives five points.

The winner of the round is the player with the higher total score.

Three rounds should be played, each time with a different target.

SETS AND SEQUENCES

SETS, COUNTING, ADDITION, MULTIPLICATION
Two or more players
This is essentially the game of Rummy applied to the teaching of sets, sequences, addition, and multiplication.

After shuffling the cards thoroughly, the dealer gives each player five, facedown, one at a time, proceeding from left to right. The remainder of the deck is placed facedown on the table within easy reach of all players.

Each player, in turn, draws from the top of the deck one card and then discards one card, faceup, on the table.

A discarded card can be picked up by the next player if he can use it; but once it is covered by another discarded card, it cannot be picked up by any player.

The object of the game is to get a hand consisting of one pair of cards having the same numerical value—say, two kings; two queens, or two 3s—and one set of three cards having the same numerical value—say, three 10s or three 5s. When a player has these groups in his hand, he lays them down on the table, and the round is over.

The player with a winning hand scores thirty-five points. In addition, he and all the other players score points for any set that they have in their hands by adding up the numerical values of the cards in the set. For example, if a player with a winning hand had three kings, he would score $3 \times 13 = 39$. In addition, if he had two 10s, he would score $2 \times 10 = 20$. His total score would then be $35 + 39 + 20 = 94$. Another player with three queens would score $3 \times 12 = 36$; one with three jacks would score $3 \times 11 = 33$.

Several rounds should be played. The first player to score two hundred points is the winner.

The challenge can be increased by giving each player seven cards and making the object of the game to produce a hand with three cards of one numerical value and four of another—for instance, three kings and four 10s, or three 5s and four jacks. Scoring is the same, except that a player with a winning hand receives a bonus of fifty points in addition to the total of the numerical values of the sets he holds. In this case, three hundred points are needed to win.

If each player is dealt nine cards, the winning hand may consist either wholly of sets — say, three 9s and four kings — or a combination of a set with a sequence of three or four cards of the same suit. Hence, a player may win the round with a hand containing four 5s and a sequence consisting of 6, 7, and 8 of hearts, or with a hand consisting of four 5s and three 2s. Scoring is the same.

SAD CASINO

SUBTRACTION, ADDITION, DIVISION

Two, three, or four players

One player acts as dealer for each game. He gives four cards to each player and four to the table, dealt one at a time from left to right. The cards on the table are dealt faceup; those given to the players, facedown.

Looking at his hand and at the table, the first player tries to find something to *take* — for example, two cards, a 5 and a 4, that *add* up to a card in his hand, say 9 — or something to *match* — like a jack on the table that matches a jack in his hand. Let us assume that he takes a 5 and a 4 with a 9 from his hand. He puts all three cards facedown on the table before him. He may play only one card from his hand each turn.

Suppose that a jack and a 5 are left on the table as a result, and the second player removes the jack because it matches a jack in his hand. He, too, places both cards facedown on the table before him.

Now the third player, if he has a 3 in his hand, can *match* the 3 on the table and *sweep* the table, because there will be no cards left on it. A clean sweep of all the cards on the table adds one point, which is immediately noted on the player's scorecard.

If, when a player's turn comes, there are no cards left on the table because they have all been swept off, he must put one of his cards on the table.

In addition to matching, taking, and sweeping, a player may *build,* by using one card from his hand and some cards from the table. For example, if he has in his hand a 9 and a 1, and there is an 8 on the table, he may put the 1 on the 8 and say, "1 + 8 = 9." He then awaits his next turn, in the hope of taking the two cards.

However, another player may, in the meantime, when his turn comes, *capture* the "build" if he has in his hand a card with a numerical value equal to the sum of the cards being built on the table. So, in this particular case, a player with a 9 may capture the 8 + 1 on the table before the builder himself has a chance to take these cards.

Then, too, a player may build on top of his opponent's "build." For instance, if a build of 8 + 1 = 9 is on the table, a player may put a 1 on top of it and say, "Now I make it 9 + 1 = 10." This new "build" in turn may be captured by another player.

To protect a "build" from being captured, a player can reinforce it. Thus, if a player has put a 1 from his hand on an 8 on the table in order to build 9, and if he sees that a 6 and a 3 are also on the table, he may during the same turn put this pair on top of his "build." This reinforced "build" is then safe against a higher "build"—say, $9 + 1 = 10$—but it is not safe against a capture by some other player's 9.

The game continues in this way until all the hands are used up. The dealer then gives four more cards to each player, but this time he gives none to the table. At the end of the game, the player who takes in the last card will clear the table of all unused cards.

The player collecting the most cards wins three points. The one with the most spades wins an additional point. Two points are earned for the 10 of diamonds (which is called Big Casino) and one point is scored for the 2 of spades (which is called Little Casino). Each ace collected counts one point. And, as stated before, one point is added for a clean sweep of the table.

The higher or highest score wins, or more games can be played until one player scores twenty-five points.

Added excitement can be given to this game if, when the cards are dealt, the rest of the pack is laid facedown on the table within easy reach of all the players. Then, after each player has made his move, he draws one card from the top of the pack, thus always having four cards in his hand.

One complete game played like this could be called "Add Casino"; it is merely the warm-up for SAD Casino, in which the players are permitted to use Subtraction, Addition, or Division. Thus, with an 8 and a 2, a player might operate as follows: $8 - 2 = 6$; $8 + 2 = 10$; $8 \div 2 = 4$. So if a player has made a "build" of $8 + 2 = 10$, an opponent may put a 3 on it and say, "$10 - 3 = 7$," or he may put a 5 on it and say, "$\frac{8 + 2}{5} = 2$." (Answers obtained by division should always be rounded to the nearest whole number.)

CASINO BASEBALL

ADDITION, SUBTRACTION, MULTIPLICATION, DIVISION

Two or more players   Marker objects

Paper and pencil

Add two jokers to a deck of cards. These are to be used as pinch hitters.

Four cards are dealt, one at a time, to each player and to the table. The cards on the table are laid facedown.

The rules of SAD Casino, above, are followed, with the players taking in cards of the same numerical value and building up values by means of addition, subtraction, multiplication, and division. But the scoring and the order in which players take turns are as in baseball.

To score the game, draw a diamond and use checkers or other objects to mark the position of the players at the various bases.

The first player is the batter up. If he collects no cards, he has struck out, but he is entitled to three outs for one inning before the next player gets his turn at bat. For every two cards a player collects, he scores one base. If he collects three cards—for example, 2 + 3 = 5—he scores a two-base hit. Collecting four cards scores a three-base hit; and when five or more cards are collected, this is equivalent to a home run. For a "build," there is no penalty; the player gets a chance to collect the cards and to score their value.

If a player draws a joker, he puts it aside. He is now entitled to exchange any card in his hand for a new card drawn from the unused ones in the pack on the table.

Nine innings should be played.

BASEBALL MADS

MULTIPLICATION, ADDITION, DIVISION, SUBTRACTION

Two or more players

After shuffling the cards, place three faceup on the table. These three cards—let us say they are 4, king (= 13), and 7—represent the second player, who is in the field, while the first player is at bat.

Now the first player turns up two cards—say, queen and 3.

The second player must now try to put the batter out by the use of MADS (Multiplication, Addition, Division, and Subtraction). With the queen and a 3, here is what he does:

$M:$ $12 \times 3 = 36$
$A:$ $12 + 3 = 15$
$D:$ $12 \div 3 = 4$
$S:$ $12 - 3 = 9$

Since 4 is in the field, and $12 \div 3 = 4$, the second player has put the first player out. The latter continues until three men are out. Then the second player goes to bat.

Suppose a batter turns up a 5 and a 3. Using MADS gives the fielder the following results:

$M:$ $5 \times 3 = 15$
$A:$ $5 + 3 = 8$
$D:$ $5 \div 3 = 1\ 2/3 = 2$
$S:$ $5 - 3 = 2$

Since none of these numbers is in the field, the batter is safe on first. A baseball diamond can be drawn to keep track of the players with the aid of markers, which can be moved from base to base.

If the same player then turns up an 8, which matches the result of $5 + 3 = 8$ previously achieved, he steals two bases and advances from first to third. Had he picked up a 7, which is one less than 8, he would steal one base and advance from first to second. Any number turned up which is one more or one less than any of the MADS numbers allows the player to advance one base. Any other number turned up puts the man on base out.

When three men are out, the next player is at bat, and new cards are drawn for the field after all the cards have been collected and shuffled.

A double or even a triple out is sometimes possible. For example, if a queen, an ace, and a 7 are in the field, and the batter turns up a 4 and a 3, his inning is over, because there are three out: $4 \times 3 = 12$; $4 - 3 = 1$; and $4 + 3 = 7$. If only two cards in the field are the same as the results of using MADS on the batter's cards, then it is two out, or a double play.

On the other hand, if a batter turns up two cards of the same suit, he gets, as a bonus, a two-base hit.

Play nine innings.

CONCENTRATION

ADDITION, MULTIPLICATION
Two or more players
In this game, the jack counts as 11, the queen as 12, and the king as 13.

After shuffling the cards, lay them facedown, separately, on the table or the floor, helter-skelter.

The first player chooses a target number from 2 through 26. Suppose he chooses 9. This will be the target for all the players.

He next picks up any two cards and holds them up for all to see. If they add up to 9 — say, a 3 and a 6, or a 5 and a 4 — he sets them aside in a pile and gets another chance to draw two cards, one at a time, from those lying facedown on the table. If his cards do not add up to 9, he puts them back, facedown, where they were before, and the next player gets his turn to draw two cards. All players try to remember where the two cards laid down by the first player are located and what numbers are on them, because they may be needed later. Let us suppose that a 2 and a 5 have been put back, facedown, on the table by the first player.

The second player also tries to reach a total of 9 with the two cards he has picked up. Suppose he first picks up a 4. Remembering that a 5 was laid down by the first player and recalling where it was put, he may pick this card up from the table, show it to the other players, and, adding it to his 4, make 9 and lay both cards aside in a pile of his own. He then gets a second chance to draw two cards from the table, always picking up one at a time. At all times a card that is picked up from the table must be shown to the other players in order to give them an opportunity to memorize its location in case it is put down again.

The game proceeds in this way until the last card has been picked up from the table. The winner is the player with the greatest number of cards in his pile.

In successive rounds, different targets can be set, and the difficulty of the game can be increased by having the players draw three cards in succession. In that case, the target numbers should be raised correspondingly.

Finally, the target number can be the product of the cards picked up from the table. This variation, too, requires an increase in the target numbers.

8

GAMES WITH DICE AND DOMINOES

Two thousand years before playing cards were invented, dice were already popular. The impulse to play with dice and dominoes can be turned to educational advantage with the games in this chapter. A few of them may require, in addition, graph paper, pencils, and checkers, as indicated under the title of the game.

PRECISE DICE

ADDITION, SUBTRACTION, MULTIPLICATION

Two or more players   Dice

The first time around, each player, in turn, rolls the dice and notes as his score the sum of the two numbers he turns up.

The second time around, each player subtracts the smaller from the larger of the two numbers he rolls when his turn comes. He adds the difference to his score on the first round.

The third time around, each player calculates his score by multiplying the two numbers he rolls and adding the product to his previous score.

The fourth time around, each player performs all three operations — addition, subtraction, and multiplication — on the two numbers he rolls, and adds the results to his previous score. This is his final score. In case of a tie between two or more players, a fifth round should be played to determine the winner.

FIREMAN UP THE LADDER

ADDITION, SUBTRACTION

Two or more players   Paper and pencil

Dice

People on the twenty-fifth floor of a burning building are impatiently awaiting rescue by the first fireman to scale the ladder from the street. Who will the rescuer be?

First, set up your ladder, as shown here, with the rungs marked off to reach up to twenty-five.

The first player rolls the dice. He may add or subtract the two numbers he turns up. Thus, if he rolls a 5 and a 2, he may add them to get 7 or subtract the 2 from the 5

to get 3. If he chooses to add, he draws a line on the
seventh floor and marks it with his initial — say, A.

Now the second player rolls the dice. He gets a 2 and a 3.
He chooses to add them to get 5. Since $7 + 5 = 12$, he

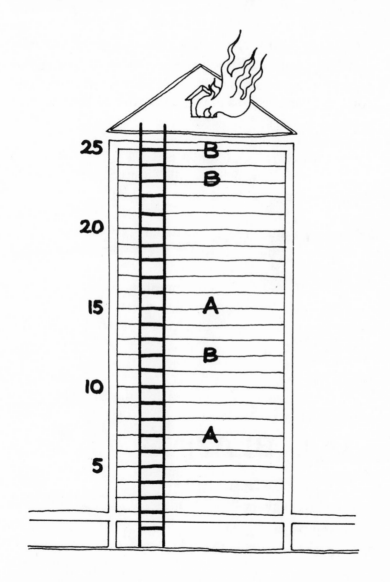

draws a line along the twelfth floor and labels it with his initial — say, B.

If A now gets $2 + 1 = 3$, he climbs up to $12 + 3 = 15$ and marks the fifteenth floor accordingly, as shown in the illustration.

If B rolls a 6 and a 2, he can add them to get 8 and add this to A's 15 to reach the twenty-third story.

The winner is the first player to reach the twenty-fifth floor.

Suppose A now rolls a 6 and a 1. $6 + 1 = 7$, which is too much. $6 - 1 = 5$, which is still too much. He needs 2, which he cannot get with these numbers. So he passes.

If B now rolls a 5 and a 3, he can subtract the 3 from the 5 and get the 2 he needs to win the game.

A player who rolls a double number — two 3s, two 5s, etc. — can score their sum or their difference (whichever is most to his advantage) and take an extra turn.

TRAIL BLAZING

ADDITION, SUBTRACTION
Two or more players   Dice
Paper and pencil
Prepare a twenty-five-box square as here illustrated.

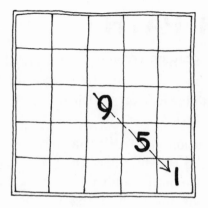

The first player rolls the dice. He can either add the two numbers he turns up or subtract the smaller from the larger. Whichever he does, he enters the result anywhere he likes on the pattern. Thus, if he rolls a 6 and a 3 and decides to enter their sum, 9, he places it in one of the boxes, as shown here.

The second player does the same. If he rolls a 4 and a 1, he could enter their sum, 5, or their difference (4–1), which is 3, in any box he likes. The object of the game is to blaze a trail of three or more connected boxes whose numbers add up to 15. In this game, the second player chose to place a 5 below and to the right of the box with the 9.

The player who succeeded in getting a 1 to complete the trail shown here, in which the numbers in the boxes add up to 15, was the winner of this game.

If a player rolls two numbers that are the same, such as two 3s, he gets an additional chance to roll the dice.

MATH PATH

ADDITION, SUBTRACTION, MULTIPLICATION, DIVISION

Two or more players   Dice

Paper and pencil

In this variation of Trail Blazing, the players may perform on the two numbers they roll any of the operations of arithmetic — addition, subtraction, multiplication, or division — in deciding on the number to be entered in a box in the pattern to make a "math path." Consequently, the "math path" must lead to a higher number than 15 — say, 21, 31, 43, and so forth.

For example, a player rolling a 5 and a 2, could multiply them to get 10, add them to get 7, subtract the 2 from the 5 to get 3, or divide the 5 by the 2 to get 2 1/2, which would be rounded off to 3. He could choose any of these results that suited his needs in making a "math path."

In all other respects, this game is played just like Trail Blazing.

THE SNAKE

DIVISION

Two or more players   Paper and pencil

Dice   Colored disks

The object of this game is to work your way from the snake's mouth, which is marked Start on the accompany-

FINISH

The Snake
(for numbers 2, 3, and 5)

ing pictures, all the way through his winding body to his tail, which is marked Finish.

First, draw a snake. (Use the illustration marked for the numbers 2, 3, and 5.)

Several disks of three different colors corresponding to these numbers—say, red for 2, yellow for 3, and green for 5—should be thrown into a grab bag. Each player draws one disk. These three numbers will serve as divisors.

The dividends will be the numbers in the sections of the snake's body. Each player, in turn, rolls a single die. The number he turns up is the number of sections he moves along the body of the snake. For example, if the first player rolls a 2, he moves his disk two sections from the Start. This will land him in the section marked 7. If he has a red disk, which is valued at 2, he finds that 7 is not divisible by 2. He must therefore move back to a section that is a multiple of 2 or go back to the Start. In this case, he will have to leave his disk at the starting point. He has made no progress at all.

Suppose that the second player rolls a 6. He moves six sections from the starting point to the number 10. Since he has a yellow disk, which is valued at 3, and since 10 is not divisible by 3, he will have to move back to the first section with a multiple of 3—in this case, the first section, which contains the number 3.

Continue in this way until one player has reached the Finish line. He wins the round and scores five points. Fifteen points are needed to win the game.

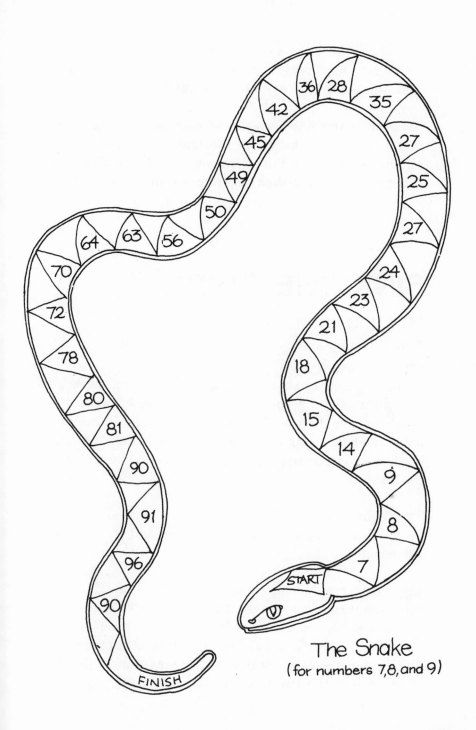

The Snake
(for numbers 7, 8, and 9)

If a player lands in a section where another player already has his disk, he must move back to a section containing a multiple of his color number.

After one game has been played with the numbers 2, 3, and 5, use the snake in the illustration marked for the numbers 7, 8, and 9. Play the game in the same way, but this time give the disks these number values.

SINK THE SHIP

PLOTTING POINTS ON A GRAPH

Two or more players   Paper and pencil
Dice

Prepare a thirty-six-box square, as shown, with a vertical axis and a horizontal axis marked off with the numbers from 1 through 6, and insert at random in six boxes the letter A, in five boxes the letter B, in four boxes the letter C, in three boxes the letter D, and in two boxes the letter S.

The As are aircraft carriers, the Bs are battleships, the Cs are cruisers, the Ds are destroyers, and the Ss are submarines.

Each player gets a turn at rolling the dice. The two numbers turned up represent the coordinates of each of two boxes, depending on which number is used as the extent of the vertical axis and which is interpreted as the limit of the horizontal axis. The player must decide which one of the two boxes to "strike" (cross out); the object is to sink as many ships as possible. If a ship is in both boxes, he can choose the box he wants to strike according to the point value of sinking the ship: one point for an aircraft carrier, two points for a battleship, three points for a cruiser, four points for a destroyer, and five points for a submarine.

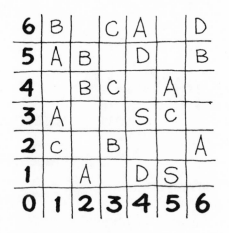

Suppose, for example, that a player rolls a 5 and a 1. He can choose either vertical 5, horizontal 1, which will land him on an aircraft carrier, counting only one point, or horizontal 5, vertical 1; which will land him on a submarine, counting five points. Naturally, he will choose the latter. Of course, if "doubles" (for example, two 6s) are rolled, he will have only one choice.

If a player sinks a ship, he scores the value of the ship and gets another chance to roll the dice. If he hits a ship that has already been sunk—marked with an X in the box—or if he hits a blank box, he loses his turn to the next player.

The game can be made easier by using dice of different colors — a black die for the horizontal axis, a white one for the vertical. The game can be made harder by using a larger square with more boxes and fewer ships to sink. The point values can also be increased.

When all the ships have been sunk, the game ends. The winner is the player with the greatest number of points.

LOCUS-POCUS

PLOTTING POINTS, ADDITION, MULTIPLICATION
Two or more players
Dice   Graph paper and pencil
Each player prepares a square of thirty-six boxes. (If only two or three are playing, each may play with two or three such squares.) He numbers the vertical columns in each square, beginning with the column at the ex-

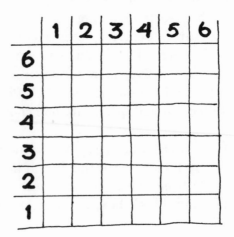

treme left, from 1 through 6 in the spaces directly above the top row of boxes; and he likewise numbers the horizontal rows in each square, beginning with the lowest, from 1 through 6 in the spaces to their left, as illustrated below. The parent or the teacher also prepares a master chart in this way.

Next, each player makes, in every one of his squares, three designs consisting of three adjacent boxes in each case, arranged in any desired pattern, by drawing the two diagonals in each of these boxes, as shown here.

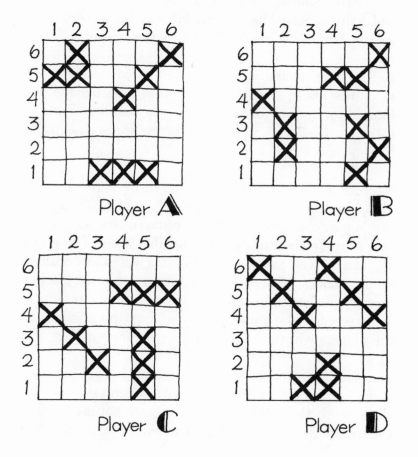

There is room at this stage for much creativity, since over one hundred such three-box patterns may be made in a thirty-six-box square.

Two pairs of dice are needed, one red, the other white. Each player, when his turn comes, should receive one red die and one white die.

The first player now rolls the dice. The number turned up on the red die indicates the horizontal locus of the box he has hit—that is, the column number shown at the top of the square; while the number turned up on the white die denotes the vertical locus of the box—that is, its row number shown at the left of the square.

Each player, including the one who rolled the dice, now examines his square or squares to see whether the box located by the numbers turned up on the dice is one of those included in one or more of his three designs. If it is, he checks the box.

Suppose, for example, that the first throw is red 3, white 1. A box three columns to the right and in the lowest row is part of a design included in the square of Player A and in the square of Player D as illustrated. These two players, as well as others having this box in any of their designs, check it, as shown, and the parent or the teacher inserts this box in his own square (which begins empty) as a record of the game and a check on the accuracy of the players who may later claim credit for winning.

The game continues, with each player taking his turn throwing the dice, until one player, finding that he has checked all three boxes in one or more patterns in his squares, yells, "Locus-Pocus!" The parent or the teacher checks his claim, and, if it is found correct, he is declared the winner of the round. If he is the only winner, he scores twenty-five points. If there are two winners, each scores ten points; three winners score eight points each; and in the rare instance when there are four or more winners, each scores five points.

By way of bonus, each winner of a round rolls the dice and scores, in addition, the sum and the product of the throw. For instance, the winner might roll red 3, white 2 (or vice versa). He would score $(3 \times 2) + (3 + 2) = 6 + 5 = 11$, over and above his score for winning the round.

Several rounds, each with different patterns in the players' squares, should be played. Depending on the number of players, the goal of the game might be one hundred or two hundred points.

GOLF

ADDITION, SUBTRACTION, MULTIPLICATION, DIVISION, PLOTTING POINTS ON A GRAPH

Two or more players   Dice

Small buttons or   Graph paper and pencil
   grains of rice

First, let us make our golf course, one hole at a time. Prepare a set of coordinates by marking off on graph paper a vertical axis and a horizontal axis and inserting a 0 and a little pennant in any one of the boxes, as shown in the illustration. This box will be the first hole.

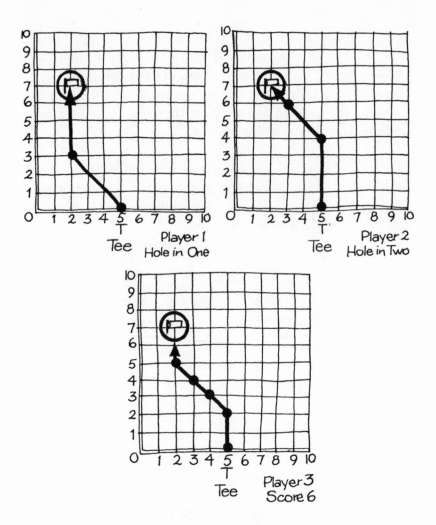

Player 1
Hole in One

Tee

Player 2
Hole in Two

Tee

Player 3
Score 6

Tee

Next, choose a tee-off point at random on the horizontal axis.

Now, each player, in turn, rolls the dice and performs on the two numbers he turns up any arithmetical operation — addition, subtraction, multiplication, or division — that will result in a number he can use in counting off the boxes from the tee-off point in any direction — to the left, to the right, straight up, diagonally leftward, or diagonally rightward — to the first hole.

For example, using the diagram shown here, the first player may roll a 4 and a 3. Since $4 + 3 = 7$, he gets a hole in one by moving three boxes diagonally leftward and four straight up and into the first hole.

If the second player rolls a 4 and a 2, he can choose to add them and use their sum, 6, to advance, as shown, four boxes straight up and two diagonally leftward. And if, on a second roll of the dice, he gets a 6 and a 5, he can choose to subtract the 5 from the 6 and use the difference, 1, to advance one box into the first hole, thereby scoring a hole in two.

Let us say that the third player first rolls a 2 and a 1, adds them, and moves up two and diagonally leftward one box. On his second roll, he turns up 5 and 4, subtracts the 4 from the 5, and advances the difference, one box, diagonally leftward. On his third roll of the dice, he gets a 1 and a 1, which he adds, using their sum to advance one box diagonally leftward and one box straight upward. His next two rolls — a 5 and a 1, and a 6 and a 2 — cannot be used in any way to advance him the one box he needs to reach the first hole. As he is allowed no more than five rolls of the dice for any one hole, he scores 6.

The small buttons or grains of rice are used to cover the boxes reached in the process of moving toward the hole.

The players now proceed to the second hole, which is placed elsewhere on the course. They choose a different tee-off point and follow the same procedure as shown for the first hole.

The player with the lowest total score after a given number of holes have been played is the winner.

To make the game even more interesting, hazards can be drawn on the course by shading certain boxes either individually or in groups. The players must then avoid these hazards or suffer penalties such as extra strokes, rolls, or points.

CONTACT

ADDITION, SUBTRACTION, MULTIPLICATION, DIVISION

Two or more players   Paper and pencil
Dice
Small buttons or grains
  of rice

Prepare a twenty-box oblong as illustrated below and enter into the boxes the numbers 1, 2, 3, 4, 5, 6, 7, 8, 9,

1	2	3	4
5	6	7	8
9	10	11	12
15	16	18	20
24	25	30	36

10, 11, 12, 15, 16, 18, 20, 24, 25, 30, and 36, in any desired arrangement.

Select a number at random—say, 10—and cover this with some marker, such as a small button or grain of rice.

The first player now rolls the dice and can perform on the two numbers he turns up any arithmetical operation—addition, subtraction, multiplication, or division—that will result in a number in a box that touches the covered number. For example, if he rolls a 5 and a 3, he can multiply them to get 15, which is in a box that touches the covered box. In that case, he places his marker over the box with 15. There are now two covered boxes, 10 and 15.

The next player may roll a 2 and a 1. No matter how these are combined ($2 + 1 = 3$; $2 \times 1 = 2$; $2 - 1 = 1$; $2 \div 1 = 2$), the result will not be a number in a box that touches either of the covered boxes. So the second player must pass.

If the following player rolls a 6 and a 3, he can add them to get 9, which is in a box that touches both covered boxes. For every covered box contacted by a player, he scores one point. So this player scores two points. It is possible for a player to contact as many as three covered boxes.

If a player incorrectly passes, any other player who calls out his mistake can cover the number as his own and score accordingly.

The game ends when all the numbers are covered. The player with the higher or highest score is the winner.

FACTOR EXTRACTOR

MULTIPLICATION, DIVISION

Two or more players   Paper and pencil
Dice

The product of two or more numbers has these numbers as its factors. Thus, 27 has as its factors 9 and 3, because $9 \times 3 = 27$. Of course, 27 is also divisible by itself (27) and by 1, but for the purposes of this game 1 is not considered a factor nor is any number considered a factor of itself.

One red die and one black die are needed. The number turned up by the red die should be multiplied by ten and added to the number turned up by the black die when both are rolled at once. Thus red 3, black 2 is equivalent to 32.

Each player writes on a piece of paper the eight numbers 2, 3, 4, 5, 6, 7, 8, and 9. These are the factors.

The first player now rolls the dice. Let us say he rolls red 3, black 6 or 36. Seeing that 2, 3, 4, 6, and 9 are all factors of 36, he crosses out these numbers on his paper, so that it looks like this: 2̸, 3̸, 4̸, 5, 6̸, 7, 8, 9̸.

The next player now rolls the dice. If he turns up red 2, black 4, or 24, he can cross out the numbers 2, 3, 4, 6, and 8 on his paper, so that it looks like this: 2̸, 3̸, 4̸, 5, 6̸, 7, 8̸, 9.

The game is continued in this way until one player has crossed out all the numbers on his paper. He is the winner.

FRACTION EXTRACTION

RECOGNIZING DECIMAL EQUIVALENTS
OF FRACTIONS

Two or more players   Paper and pencil
Dice

Each player writes on his paper the following twenty-two numbers: 1.00, .50, .33 1/3, .25, .20, .16 2/3, 2.00, .66 2/3, .40, 3.00, 1.50, .75, .60, 4.00, 1.33 1/3, 1.20, 5.00, 2.50, 1.66 2/3, 1.25, .83 1/3, and 6.00.

One red die and one black die are needed for this game. The red die will turn up the numerator, and the black die the denominator, of a fraction. Thus, red 3, black 2 is equivalent to 3/2 or 1 1/2. The decimal equivalent of this is 1.50. Red 2, black 3 is equivalent to 2/3 or .66 2/3.

Each player, in turn, rolls the dice, makes his fraction, gives its decimal equivalent, and crosses it out on his paper. So if a player rolls red 3, black 4, or 3/4, he crosses out .75.

One point is scored for each number crossed out. A bonus of five points is scored if a double number, equivalent in every case to 1.00 (1/1, 2/2, etc.), is turned up. The winner is the player who scores a hundred points first.

DECIMAL DESIGNS

RECOGNIZING DECIMAL EQUIVALENTS
OF FRACTIONS

Two or more players   Paper and pencil
Dice

This game is a variation of Fraction Extraction, the preceding game, and is played in exactly the same way, but the decimal numbers are inserted in the boxes of a twenty-five-box square. They should be placed at random, with three boxes left empty.

The crossing out of the decimals is done by drawing diagonal lines through the squares in which they are inserted. A round is won when a player has crossed out the decimals in three adjacent boxes, whether diagonally, vertically, or horizontally, or in any other shape.

BANKER

ADDITION, SUBTRACTION, MULTIPLICATION, DIVISION, MAKING CHANGE WITH DECIMAL COINAGE

Two or more players   Chips
Dice

The object of this game is to exchange a certain amount of money for a definite number of coins and bills. For example, to make seven dollars with six coins or bills, you need one five-dollar bill, one one-dollar bill, and four quarters.

Each player rolls the dice twice. The sum of the two dice on the first roll determines the amount of money to be exchanged; thus, if 4 and 3 are rolled, seven dollars must be exchanged. The second roll of the dice determines the number of bills or coins or both that are needed; again, the two numbers rolled are added. So if a 5 and a 4 are turned up, nine bills or coins are required. To make seven dollars with nine bills or coins, use one five-dollar bill, one one-dollar bill, two quarters, and five dimes.

Chips of different colors can be used to represent pennies, nickels, dimes, quarters, halves, dollar bills, and five-dollar bills.

Every exchange must be equivalent in money value. But it is not always possible to achieve this with a given number of coins or bills. If a player does succeed in making exact change, he scores five points. Otherwise, he loses one point for every coin or bill needed to make exact change that is more or less than the number called for. So if nine coins or bills are called for, and only eight are needed, the player loses one point off the five that would be a perfect score and gets only four. Similarly, if nine coins or bills are called for, and ten are needed to make exact change, the player gets only four points or one less than what he would get for a perfect score.

A player gets a bonus of two points if he rolls a double number and five points if both rolls yield a double number.

The winner is the first to score one hundred points.

POKER DICE

ADDITION, SUBTRACTION, MULTIPLICATION, DIVISION, SETS

Two or more players   Dice

The object of the game is to role dice to get combinations like those in poker—a pair, three of a kind, or four of a kind. (Straights and flushes are not used in this game.)

Each player rolls one die five times. Using as many of the resulting figures as he can, he then tries by addition, subtraction, multiplication, or division to make them equal to the same number as many times as possible.

For example, suppose that a player throws 5, 6, 2, 3, and 4. He can use all five of these integers to get three of a kind (2s): $6 - 4$, $5 - 3$, and 2. His score would then be $(3 \times 2) + 5$ (the number of integers used) $= 11$.

Another player might throw, 6, 6, 5, 2, and 1. He could use four of these integers to get three of a kind (6s): 6, 6, and $5 + 1$. His score would be $(3 \times 6) + 4 - 2$ (the integer not used, which is always subtracted from the total) $= 20$.

Still another player might throw 3, 3, 2, 1, and 3. Using all five of these numbers, he could get four of a kind (3s): $3 = 3 = 3 = 2 + 1$. His score would be $(4 \times 3) + 5 = 17$.

The player attaining the higher or highest score after each player has had ten turns wins the game.

SIX CLICKS

ADDITION
Two, three, or four players   Dominoes
In this game six clicks for two reasons: first, because each player starts with six dominoes, which he draws from a pile of them scattered facedown on the table; and secondly, because, when his turn comes, he must use one of his dominoes to make a sum of six when one of

the numbers on his domino is added to one of the numbers at either end of the dominoes arranged faceup on the table.

Each player keeps his set of six dominoes hidden from the other players.

The first player puts one of his pieces on the table faceup. Let us say it shows a 3 and a 4.

Now the second player must find either a 3 or a 2 on his dominoes, in order to make the sum of 6: 4 + 2 or 3 + 3 = 6. In this game, he places a 3,5 domino as shown in the illustration.

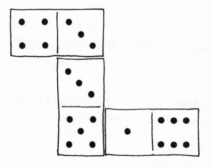

The next player must find either a 1 to add to the 5 or a 2 to add to the 4. In this game he adds a 1,6 domino as illustrated.

If a player has no dominoes he can use, he must draw from the pool on the table until he finds what he is looking for. If he still cannot move after drawing every domino from the table, he passes the turn to the next player.

The game continues in this way until one player has used up all of his dominoes or a stalemate occurs in which no one can move.

Each player scores the sum of the two numbers on the domino he places on the table. So if a player puts down a 6,2 domino, he scores $6 + 2 = 8$. A bonus of ten points is scored by the player who uses up all his dominoes.

Winner is the player with the higher or highest score.

WON BY ONE

SUBTRACTION

Two, three, or four players   Dominoes

This variation of Six Clicks is won by one because the numbers on the matching dominoes must make a difference of one.

Thus, in the game illustrated below, the 6 is laid against the 5 because $6 - 5 = 1$, and the 2 is placed against the 1 because $2 - 1 = 1$.

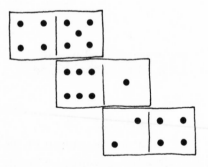

In all other respects the game is played and scored like Six Clicks.

118

USE TWOS

SUBTRACTION

Two, three, or four players   Dominoes

In this variation you use twos because the numbers on the matching dominoes must differ always by just two.

For example, in the game illustrated below, the 3 is put next to the 5 because $5 - 3 = 2$, and the 2 is set against the 4 because $4 - 2 = 2$.

In every other respect this variation is played just like Six Clicks and is scored in the same way.

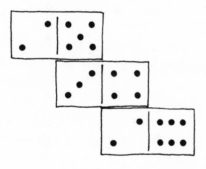

MADS DOMINOES

MULTIPLICATION, ADDITION, DIVISION, SUBTRACTION

Two, three, or four players   Dominoes

In this variation, each player scores twice with every move he makes—once from the amount of the difference between the numbers on the matching dominoes and again from the sum of the numbers on the domino he lays down.

The first score corresponds directly to the difference between the numbers that are placed next to each other when a domino is put down on the table: one point if the difference is 1, two points if the difference is 2, and so on, to six points if the difference is 6. If the two numbers are the same, so that the difference is 0, the player who matches them scores five points.

Here is how the first score would be calculated in a typical game illustrated below. The first difference is $6 - 3 = 3$; the second is $5 - 5 = 0$, which scores five points; and the third is $2 - 0 = 2$.

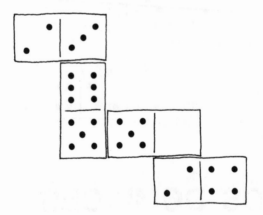

In addition, a player scores one point if the sum of the two numbers on the domino he lays on the table equals 3, 4, or 5. If the sum is divisible by three, he scores two points. If the sum is a multiple of 4, he scores three points. If the sum is a multiple of 5, he scores five points. And if the sum is 7 or 11, he scores two points.

Here is how the additional scores would be calculated in the game illustrated below. The first player adds the 3 and the 6 to get 9, which is a multiple of 3. So he scores two points. The second player adds the 6 and the 4, to get 10, which is a multiple of 5 (5 × 2 = 10). So he scores five points. The third player adds 5 and 6 to get 11 and scores two points. And the fourth player adds 6 and 2, to get 8, which is a multiple of 4 (4 × 2 = 8). So he scores three points.

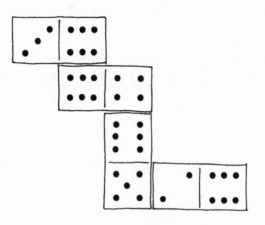

Each player then adds both scores for his move. The first player to attain one hundred points is the winner.

HIGH-LOW

ADDITION, SUBTRACTION

Two or more players   Dominoes

Scatter a set of dominoes facedown on the table.

Each player selects four. He adds up the high numbers and then the low numbers on the dominoes. His score is the difference between these two sums.

For example, if a player selected the dominoes shown below, he would first add $5 + 4 + 6 + 6 = 21$. (The blank is a joker and may be substituted for any number.) Then he would add the low numbers: $2 + 3 + 2 + 5 = 12$. Finally, he would subtract: $21 - 12 = 9$. This is his score.

Continue in this way until all the dominoes have been drawn. The player with the higher or highest total score is the winner.

9

GAMES WITH PREPARED MATERIALS

Every one of the games in this chapter requires a combination of various materials. Whether graph paper, coins, dominoes, dice, adhesive tabs, playing cards, colored crayons, or a checkerboard, the necessary materials listed for each game are easily available. The few minutes devoted to setting up a chart, drawing a diagram, affixing stickers to the backs of playing cards and writing on them with a felt marking pen, or otherwise getting everything ready can prove most rewarding. Often the players can help with the preparations and learn about arithmetic in the process.

FIGURE IT OUT

RECOGNITION AND IDENTIFICATION
OF GEOMETRIC FIGURES

Two, three, or four players   Adhesive tabs
Playing cards   Felt marking pen

Remove four cards from a deck, and attach an adhesive tab to the back of each of the remaining forty-eight cards. Then divide the cards into two packs of twenty-four each.

On the tab on each of twelve cards in one of these packs draw a different one of the following twelve geometric figures:

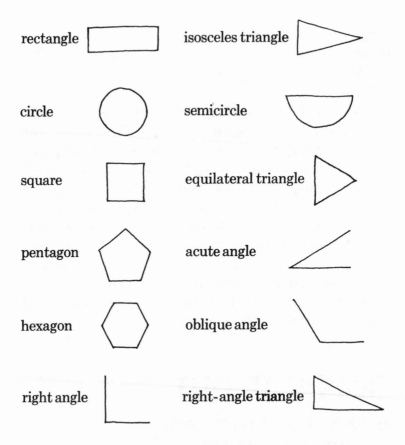

rectangle   isosceles triangle

circle   semicircle

square   equilateral triangle

pentagon   acute angle

hexagon   oblique angle

right angle   right-angle triangle

Do the same with the other twelve cards in this pack, so that each geometric figure is represented twice.

On the tabs of the twenty-four cards in the other pack write the names of these figures, so that each figure is represented twice by its name.

Now shuffle all the cards in both packs together into one pack of forty-eight. Deal five cards to each player, one at a time, from left to right. Place the remaining cards on the table faceup (tabs are therefore facedown) within easy reach of the players.

Each player first discards any cards that match each other—for example, two figures of a right angle or one figure of a right angle and the words "right angle."

The first player then draws a card from the top of the pack on the table. If he can use it to make a match with the cards remaining in his hand, he takes it and places the two matched cards faceup in a pile in front of him. If he cannot use the card he has drawn, he returns it, faceup, to the table. The next player may take this card to make a match with a card in his hand, or he may draw the top card from the deck.

The game proceeds in this fashion until one player has used up all his cards. If a stalemate occurs, the players may try trading cards. If no trades can be made, they should play another round.

One point is scored for every card laid down by a player as part of a match. Thus five matches will score ten points. The player with the higher or highest score wins.

In successive rounds, different geometric figures may be introduced: the square, the six-pointed star, the five-pointed star, the ellipse, the sector, the arc, the helix, etc., for the sake of variety and depending on the maturity of the players.

LINE-UP

ADDITION, PLOTTING POINTS ON A GRAPH

Two or more players   Paper and pencil

Dice or playing cards   Crayons

First prepare a thirty-six-box square by inserting the numbers in it at random from 1 to 36. Mark off with numbers from 1 to 6 the vertical axis and the horizontal axis as shown below.

6	1	12	6	24	30	18
5	7	2	19	13	31	25
4	20	32	26	8	15	36
3	27	3	14	21	9	33
2	16	28	10	4	12	35
1	4	5	17	29	11	23
0	1	2	3	4	5	6

To determine the horizontal and vertical coordinates of the numbered boxes, the players may use either a set of playing cards with the numbers from 1 through 6 or a red die and a black die. In either case, red numbers will show how many boxes are to be counted off horizontally from zero, and the black numbers will correspond to the vertical coordinate. So if a player rolls red 3, black 2, or if he picks, from each of two stacks of cards previously set up, red 3 (hearts or diamonds) and black 2 (spades or clubs), he counts three boxes to the right and two up, landing in the box with the number 10 in our illustration. The player checks this box with the color he is using — say, red.

Each player does the same, using a differently colored crayon to identify himself as the "owner" of the box he has checked. If a player rolls or picks a pair of numbers that locate a box already occupied, either as his own or some other player's, he loses his turn.

The first player to gain ownership of three adjacent boxes, whether vertically, horizontally, or diagonally, scores the sum of all the numbers on the winning line. Any box checked that is on one of the two longest diagonals gives its owner a bonus of ten points. For example, in the game illustrated here, the player with the blue checks scored 32 + 14 + 4 = 50 + 30 more because each of his owned boxes was a major diagonal = 80. The player with the red check on 28, which is also on a major diagonal, scored ten points.

Several rounds should be played, each time with a different arrangement of the thirty-six numbers in the boxes. The player with the highest score after a given number of rounds is the winner.

EXACT RECKONING

ADDITION, SUBTRACTION, MULTIPLICATION, DIVISION, FACTORING

Two, three, or four players   Timer

Prepared cards

Each player gets ten blank index cards. Selecting any two numbers from 1 to 10, he performs on these numbers any two arithmetical operations—addition, subtraction, multiplication, or division. Using S for sum, P for product, Q for quotient, and D for difference, he puts the results on one card. Using different numbers and different sets of operations, he does the same for the other nine cards.

For example, with the numbers 9 and 3, he might put down on a card S 12, P 27, or D 6, Q 3 (meaning that their sum is 12, their product is 27, their difference is 6, and their quotient is 3). All that the card would contain would be any two of the abbreviated expressions; the computations themselves would not appear.

When all the cards have been prepared, each player shuffles his set and lays them facedown on the table. The players take turns in drawing cards from the top of one another's piles. Within a given time limit—say, a minute—a player must, from the clues given on the card, say what two numbers give these results. For example, a card with S 3, P 2—that is, representing two numbers whose sum is 3 and whose product is 2—presents a problem that can be solved only with the numbers 1 and 2: $1 + 2 = 3; 1 \times 2 = 2$.

A player scores one point for each correct solution arrived at within the time limit. If a player gives an incorrect answer or is unable to solve the problem within the given time, the player who prepared the card must provide the solution. If he does so, he scores two points. The higher or highest scorer wins the game.

EXACT WEIGHT

ADDITION, SUBTRACTION, EQUIVALENTS, FRACTIONS

Two or more players   Timer
Prepared cards

In this game the players are in the sand business. They sell packages of sand of different weights, from 5 to 15 pounds, according to the demands of their customers. The weights have to be exact.

First, prepare twenty cards, each with a different weight number: 2 ounces, 5 ounces, 11 ounces, 59 ounces, 62 ounces, 1 1/2 pounds, 2 3/4 pounds, 3 1/2 pounds, etc.

Next, after shuffling the cards, lay them out separately, faceup, on the table so that they can all be seen.

The first player is the sand seller; the second is the sand buyer. The buyer states how many pounds of sand he wants or how many ounces. For example, suppose he wants fourteen pounds. Now the seller must, within a given time, select the cards that can be used on a scale to balance a package of sand of that exact weight. He might select a combination of 9, 6, and 1: 9 pounds + 6 pounds = 15 pounds on one side of the scale to balance the package of sand + 1 pound on the other side of the scale. $15 = P + 1$. $P = 15 - 1 = 14$.

For the correct solution the seller scores one point in addition to the numerical value of the weight of sand he has sold. In this case, $14 + 1 = 15$.

The players take turns as buyers and sellers. The first to score one hundred points is the winner.

EXACT MEASURE

ADDITION, SUBTRACTION, EQUIVALENTS, FRACTIONS

Two or more players   Containers of various sizes
Prepared cards   Timer

This variation of Exact Weight is played in the same way except that the sellers must provide their customers with exact measures of liquids—pints, quarts, gallons —or solids—pecks and bushels.

For this purpose, you may use empty containers of frozen orange juice, bottles, jars, and jugs of different sizes and known or specified capacity. These will make more challenging the task of figuring out, for example, how, using 2 quarts, 5 quarts, and 8 quarts, to measure out exactly 4 quarts. Containers could be labeled 2 quarts, 3 quarts, 5 quarts, 8 quarts, 10 quarts, etc., and the cards would be prepared accordingly.

In scoring the game, follow the rules of Exact Weight.

COMBINATIONS

ADDITION, SUBTRACTION, MULTIPLICATION, DIVISION

| Two or more players | Cubes |
| Timer | Removable tapes |

For this game you will need six cubes or three pairs of dice.

Cover each of the six sides of every cube or die with removable adhesive tape. On the sides of one cube write the numbers 0, 1, 2, 3, 4, and 5; on the sides of a second, 6, 7, 8, 9, 0, and 1; prepare a third with 2, 3, 4, 5, 6, and 7; and a fourth with 8, 9, 0, 1, 2, and 3. A fifth cube should have written on its sides the symbols $+$, $-$, $\times$, $\div$, $+$, and $-$; and the sixth cube should have $\times$, $\div$, $+$, $-$, $\times$, and $\div$; so that each symbol appears three times altogether.

Each player, when his turn comes, rolls all six cubes and tries to combine the numbers and symbols he turns up into a true arithmetical statement. He scores ten points if he uses all the cubes in forming his statement, and five points if he uses only three cubes. A time limit should be set for each play.

For example, a player who rolls 9, 7, 5, 3, $+$, and $-$ could score ten points if, within the given time limit, he arranges the cubes to form the true arithmetical statement: $9 - 5 + 3 = 7$. (The sign $=$ does not appear on the cubes but is supplied by the player in the appropriate place.)

If, on the other hand, a player rolls 8, 4, 2, 3, $\div$, and $\times$, he could score five points by combining them to make the true arithmetical statement $8 \div 4 = 2$, because he would be using three of the six cubes.

The winner is the first player to score twenty-five points.

TAG

ADDITION, SUBTRACTION, MULTIPLICATION, DIVISION

Two or more players   Dice

Buttons or checkers   Paper and pencil

First, prepare a sixteen-box square and insert any numbers in the boxes at random, as in the sample shown below.

1	15	10	6
12	5	20	16
3	9	2	7
8	18	11	25

Next, select any number in a box—say, 9—and place a checker or a button in the box containing it. This is the box to be "tagged."

The first player now rolls the dice and performs on the two numbers turned up all the operations of arithmetic —addition, subtraction, multiplication, and division. For example, if he rolls a 5 and a 3, he gets $5 + 3 = 8, 5 - 3 =$

2, 5 × 3 = 15, and 5 ÷ 3 = 1 2/3. Only the numbers 8 and 2 are in boxes that touch the box with the 9. To get a higher score, the player will choose 8 rather than 2 and place his button or checker in the box containing that number. His score is now 8.

Now the next player rolls the dice. The box to be tagged is the one with the 8. If he turns up, say, a 6 and a 3, he gets 6 + 3 = 9, 6 − 3 = 3, 6 × 3 = 18, and 6 ÷ 3 = 2. Of these, 3, 9, and 18 are in boxes that touch the one containing the 8. To attain the highest score, the second player will naturally choose 18 and places his button or checker in the box with that number. This is the box to be tagged next.

If a player cannot tag the box, he scores zero, and the next player takes his turn. And if division results in a fraction, the number should be rounded out to the nearest integer.

The game continues in this way until one player scores fifty points. He is the winner.

Of course, new charts may be made with different—larger—numbers, and the winning score would be correspondingly higher.

DIVISOR DEVISER

MULTIPLICATION; DIVISION; FACTORING; RECOGNITION OF SQUARES, CUBES, ETC.
Two or more players   Timer
Prepared cards

This is a good game to play after Factor Extractor (see page 112).

Prepare thirty-five cards, each with one number taken from any of the following groups:

4, 6, 8, 9, 10
12, 14, 15, 16, 18
20, 21, 24, 27, 28
30, 32, 36, 40, 48
54, 56, 60, 64, 70
72, 80, 81, 84, 90
96, 100, 125, 144, 1000

Each group should be represented. Then shuffle the cards.

The players take turns drawing one card from the top of the deck, and within a given time limit each must find as many factors of the number he has drawn as he can. Remember that a factor is a divisor, but for this game we do not consider 1 or the number itself among the factors of a number.

Suppose, for example, that a player draws 48. He could say: $48 = 2 \times 24, 3 \times 16, 4 \times 12$, and 6×8. He scores one point for each set of factors that he can think of in the time limit — in this case, four points. He can score five points extra for a square number — for example, $25 = 5 \times 5$ — and ten points extra for a cubic number like 27 $(3 \times 3 \times 3)$. A number raised to the fourth power, like 16 $(2 \times 2 \times 2 \times 2)$, scores twenty-five points; a number raised to the fifth power, like 32 $(2 \times 2 \times 2 \times 2 \times 2)$, scores fifty points; and a number raised to the sixth power scores one hundred points.

If a player does not, within a given time limit, recognize all the possible factors and powers of the number he has drawn, the player whose turn is next may score the point values missed, provided that he states the factors and powers correctly. In any case, he takes his turn and draws a card.

The first player to attain a score of two hundred points is the winner.

FACTOR HOCKEY

MULTIPLICATION, DIVISION, FACTORING

Two players only   Playing cards
Paper and pencil   Disk

First, prepare a playing board, as indicated in the following illustration, to serve as the hockey field. The board should be at least the size of a sheet of paper or larger. A piece of cardboard used as backing will make the board more durable. The numbers on this board represent areas to which the puck—a checker, coin, or disk such as a button—is moved.

Next, each player selects a goal. Let us say that Player A has selected the goal near the 3, and that Player B has selected the goal near the 2.

After removing all kings, queens, and jacks from the deck of playing cards, shuffle the cards and place the deck facedown on the table. Position the puck in the center of the board, in the area marked C.

135

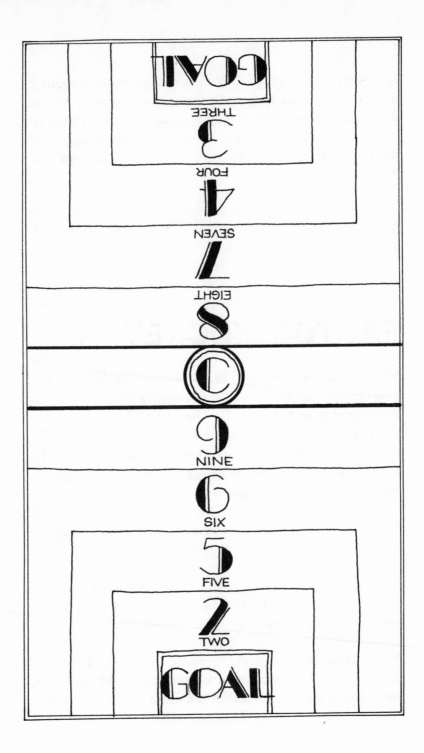

Player A starts by turning up two cards. Each card is to be treated as a digit, with the 10 counting as zero. Thus, if he turns up a 6 and a 7, his number is 67. Since Player A has chosen the goal near the 3, his factor numbers are 5, 6, and 9. As none of these is a factor of 67, he passes.

It is now Player B's turn to draw two cards from the top of the deck. Suppose he turns up a 2 and an 8, making the number 28. Since his factor numbers are 4, 7, and 8, he has two numbers, 4 and 7, that are factors of 28. He therefore moves the puck two spaces toward his goal, landing on 6. Since he was able to move the puck, he gets another chance to draw two cards. If, for example, he now draws a 5 and a 3, making 53, he cannot move forward again, because this number is not divisible by any of his factor numbers. However, since he is in "enemy" territory, he may take a "goal shot." This time, let us say, he turns up 72. Great! The number 6, where the puck is, is a factor of 72 ($12 \times 6 = 72$). So he scores one point. (Note that in the case of a goal shot, the factor where the puck sits is the only factor.)

The puck is now put back at the center of the board. Player B gets still another chance, since he scored. If, this time, he turns up a 3 and a 10, making 30, he must pass, because this number is not divisible by 4, 7, or 8.

Only goal shots are scored. So, no matter how close a player comes to the goal, he must take a goal shot to gain a point. Note that both players have smaller numbers as they come closer to the goal. This, of course, affords them more opportunity to score.

If a player chooses, he may, when his turn comes, take a goal shot. But then, if he misses, he loses his chance and must pass. It is wise to come close to the goal before risking a goal shot.

Any player drawing a 10 and another 10 has automatically scored a goal.

After all the cards in the deck have been used, shuffle them and begin again. Once the cards have been run through a second time, stop. This point marks the end of a period; the players change goals and therefore their factor numbers.

Play three periods to finish the game. The player with the higher score is the winner.

DROP IT!

ADDITION, SUBTRACTION, MULTIPLICATION, DIVISION OF FRACTIONS, WHOLE NUMBERS, EQUIVALENCES

Two or more players   Timer
Paper and pencil   Disk

Prepare a large circle like the one shown in the next illustration. Using a cardboard disk as a guide, draw several smaller circles within the large circle and insert in each of these a problem in arithmetic. In the example illustrated here, the problems involve the multiplication of fractions, but this game could be used to review the addition, subtraction, and division of both fractions and whole numbers as well as problems relating to the

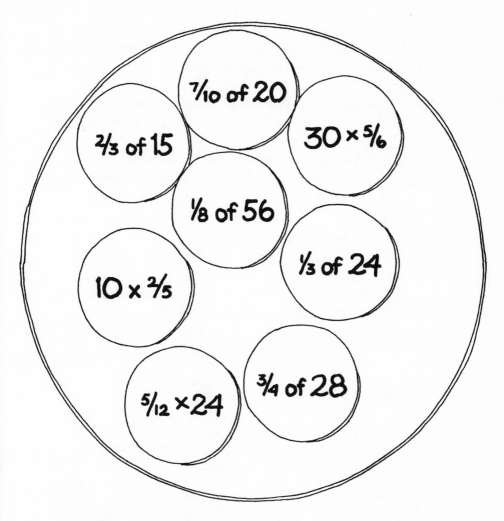

equivalences listed in the Table of Equivalents appended at the back of this book.

Each player in turn holds the disk — which could be a coin or a button — at eye level above the "target" and, after aiming, drops it. He scores the sum of the numerical values of the problems in all the circles his disk touches, provided that he works these out correctly within a given time limit. For example, if he drops the disk so that it touches the circles with $10 \times 2/5$, $1/8$ of 56, and $5/12$ of 24, he scores $4 + 7 + 10 = 21$.

The first player to score one hundred points is the winner.

Several different targets involving arithmetical problems at various levels of difficulty can be prepared.

10

PARTY GAMES

The games in this chapter are best suited for large families or gatherings, such as children's parties, groups of campers, or even classes in school. In many of them the players can be divided into teams.

For the games that are not oral, you will find the necessary materials listed under the titles.

GIANT STEP

ADDITION, SUBTRACTION, MULTIPLICATION, DIVISION, FRACTIONS, DECIMALS

Six or more players $3'' \times 5''$ cards

This game involves activity on the part of groups of children organized into teams.

First, the children produce three sets of at least twenty $3'' \times 5''$ cards. Each card in the first set should contain easy examples in addition — for example, $9 + 3$, $5 + 6 + 2$, $7 + 8 + 1$, etc. The second set should consist of cards with somewhat more difficult problems, like $57 + 9$, $65 + 26$, $19 + 18 + 5$, etc. In the third set every card should have on it a really challenging problem in addition, like $298 + 92$, $74 + 16 + 15$, $496 + 125$, etc. All the cards in the first set should be labeled A; those in the second set, B; and those in the third set, C.

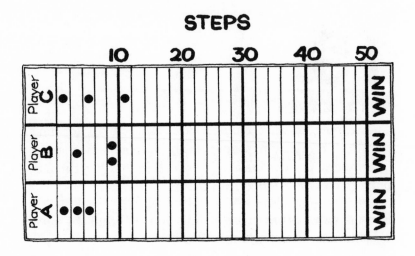

Now combine all the cards into one deck, shuffle them thoroughly, and place them facedown on the table.

The first player of the first team turns up the top card and announces the set that it is in — say, A. He then does the example, and, if he thinks he is correct, he asks, "May I take a step?" If he is right, he will be permitted to take one step forward. If he correctly does an example from a card in set B, he may advance two steps; and if he solves a problem on a card in set C, he is allowed to proceed three steps forward — the equivalent of a "giant step."

To mark progress, you may chalk out a scoreboard on the floor, as shown, indicating the starting line and the length of each step. The player or team that first reaches the finish line, which is the fiftieth step, is the winner.

After a few rounds with addition, the problems can involve subtraction, multiplication, or division. Problems can become more difficult by involving fractions or decimals.

A-RHYTHM-E-TAG

ADDITION, SUBTRACTION, MULTIPLICATION,
DIVISION, DECIMALS, FRACTIONS

Six or more players   Prepared tags

This is another active game requiring that the players be first divided into two equal teams. One team is called the Odds; and the other, the Evens.

Each member of the Odds will be tagged with a card containing an odd number different from that of any other member of his team: 1, 3, 5, 7, etc., up to a figure that depends on the number of players on the team. Similarly, each member of the Evens will display on his tag an even number distinguishing him from the rest of his teammates: 2, 4, 6, 8, etc.

The captains of the two teams choose to see who will be first to go. Let us say that the Odds go first and that No. 3 is selected to begin. He leads his group in a rhythmic pantomime: all first slap their thighs, then clap hands, next turn the wrist of the right hand, and finally turn the left wrist. No. 3 must then immediately make two true arithmetical statements that equal his number—for example, $8 - 5 = 3$; $6 \div 2 = 3$—and, addressing the Evens, must pose a problem for one of its members, a problem whose answer must be an even number—for example, $3 \times 4 = ?$

Now No. 12 of the Evens must step forward and quickly respond, "Twelve!" He then leads his team in the rhythmic pantomime, meanwhile thinking of two other true statements equaling his number. These he then makes —for instance, $9 + 3 = 12$; $24 \div 2 = 12$. Now it is his turn to throw a problem to another member of the Odds team who has not yet had a chance, a problem whose answer is an odd number—say, $10 \div 2 = ?$ And, of course, No. 5 must come forth and continue in the same way.

A team scores one point for each correct response given by a member. If a player makes a false statement or otherwise errs, the opposing team scores one point and takes over. The game continues until one team has scored a total of ten points.

This game can be made more difficult by increasing the number of mathematical statements required of each player and by requiring a greater variety of arithmetical operations. It can be played with decimals and fractions as well as whole numbers.

BACK NUMBERS

DISTINGUISHING BETWEEN GREATER AND
LESS, ODD AND EVEN; DIVISION; FACTORING

Six or more players   Numbered cards
Pins

Every player has a number pinned on his back. Each
can see the number on the back of every other player
but not on his own.

The object of the game is to find the number on one's own
back by asking, when one's turn comes, a question about
it that can be answered either yes or no. A player can
ask only one question at a time and must wait for his
turn to come again to ask another question.

Thus the first question a player asks might be: Is my
number odd or even? Later, when his turn comes again,
he might ask whether it ends in a 0, whether it is divisible by 9, whether it is less than 60, or greater than
25, or whether it is 36, and so forth.

The first player to guess his number is the winner.

MARBLE PITCH

ADDITION, MULTIPLICATION

Six or more players   Differently colored marbles
Containers

For this game you will need three containers—pots,
cans, cups, or jars—of different diameters, fifteen

marbles of one color (say, red), five of another (say, blue), three of still another (say, yellow), and two of yet another color (say, green).

Set the three containers from five to fifteen feet away from the players. The cup with the smallest diameter has a point value of 25; the container with the largest diameter has a value of 5; and the one of medium diameter has a value of 15.

The marbles of fewest number—in this case, green—have a value of 15; blue marbles, 10; yellow marbles, 5; and red marbles, 3. (The values given to the colors will depend on the number of marbles of any color being used: the fewer the marbles of any one color, the greater their point value; the more marbles of any one color, the smaller their value.)

Place all the marbles in a hat and shake them up thoroughly.

Each player, in turn, draws a marble from the hat and tosses it at the container of his choice. If he misses, he scores zero. If the marble lands in a container, he scores the value of the marble multiplied by the value of the container in which it has landed. For instance, if the blue marble lands in the container of medium diameter, the score is $10 \times 15 = 150$.

The first player to score 600 is the winner.

For young children, addition may be used rather than multiplication. In that case, if a blue marble lands in the container of medium diameter, the score is $10 + 15 = 25$.

COIN TOSS

ADDITION, SUBTRACTION, MULTIPLICATION,
DIVISION

Six or more players   Coins
Shoe box

Cut at equal intervals on the side of a shoe box holes
somewhat larger than the diameter of a quarter. Over
the first hole place the symbol +; over the second, −;
over the third, ×; and over the fourth, ÷, as illustrated
below.

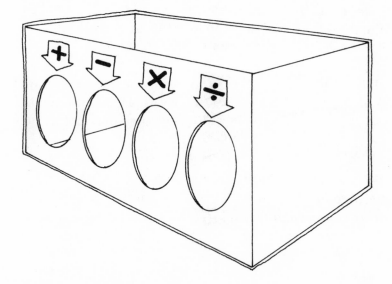

Give each player a penny, worth one point, a nickel,
worth five points; a dime, worth ten points; and a quarter, worth twenty-five points.

The players take turns standing a given distance away
from the shoe box and tossing the coins, one at a time, at
the holes of their choice. If a coin goes through a hole,

the operation indicated by the symbol above the hole is performed on the point value of the coin and the player's score so far. (A player is given one point to start with, to be used in multiplication, division, addition, or subtraction, according to the hole through which his first coin falls.)

Thus, if the first coin tossed is a quarter and it goes through the multiplication hole, the score is $25 \times 1 = 25$. Now if the player's second coin is a penny, and he misses all the holes, his score remains twenty-five. If his third coin is a nickel, and he tosses it through the addition hole, his score becomes $25 + 5 = 30$. And if his last coin, the dime, gets through the multiplication hole, his score for the round is $30 \times 10 = 300$.

Players will naturally try to avoid the subtraction and division holes because these operations would have the effect of lowering their scores, but they may not always succeed.

Scoring is cumulative from round to round and within each round for each player. The winner is the first to score a thousand points.

NUMBER-RING TOSS

ADDITION, SUBTRACTION, MULTIPLICATION, DIVISION

Six or more players   Cards
Board with holes   Quoits
Stakes

This variation of Coin Toss may be played outdoors in a back yard or a field, with the stakes driven into the ground, or indoors, with the stakes inserted into a board with holes drilled in it to accommodate them. You can also use a commercial game of quoits.

Only four stakes are needed. To begin with, give each stake a point value—say, 3, 4, 5, and 6—and mark it prominently with a card so that the players can see it from where they are standing, a given distance away from the stakes.

At the outset, give each player three rings, to be tossed, in turn, one at a time, at the stake of the player's choice. Since a player's score for each round will be the sum of the point values of the stakes he succeeds in ringing, each player will naturally aim for the stake with the highest point value—in this case, 6—but he may not always succeed in ringing it, especially if it is placed somewhat to the rear of the others or very close to the stake with the lowest point value. Continue the game until one player has scored twenty-five points. He is the winner.

The game can be made more challenging by multiplying the point values of the stakes that are ringed. Thus, if a player rings a 3 and a 4, his score is $3 \times 4 = 12$. Later, the values on the stakes can be raised—for instance, to 4, 5, 6, and 7.

Finally, the game can be played like Coin Toss if the stakes are marked with the symbols of addition (+), subtraction (−), multiplication (×), and division (÷). In that case, the stakes marked × and + should either be placed somewhat to the rear of the others in order to be more difficult to reach or should be very close to the others so that a player aiming at a high score risks having his cumulative score lowered by ringing a − or a ÷. If the game is played in this way, the three rings have to be assigned point values−say, 5 to the first, 10 to the second, and 15 to the third. To make the game even more challenging, more rings can be added and the point values increased.

STAND UP AND BE COUNTED

MULTIPLICATION

Twenty-five or more   Blackboard
   players   Index cards
Paper and pencil

This game involves the active participation of all players. It is ideal for a classroom or a campers' group.

The players are first divided into teams. In a classroom each row can be a team.

Depending on the number of players, everyone receives one or more cards to prepare for the game by writing on each card a number from 0 to 9. Five cards should be prepared for each number, that is, five 0s, five 1s, five 2s, five 3s, etc., or fifty cards in all.

After the cards have been collected and checked, they are shuffled and dealt out, two to a player. No player should have two cards of the same numerical value. If this happens, players on the same team should interchange cards.

The leader—parent or teacher—now writes an example in multiplication on the blackboard. Let us assume that the problem is 345 × 6.

All the players who have any of these four digits on their cards immediately stand up and show their cards. The leader checks them and credits each team with one point for every number used in the problem that is on the card of any member of that team.

Now the first player of the first team begins the multiplication, saying, "5 × 6 = 30." (If he makes a mistake, his team is assessed a penalty of one point.) All players with the digit 3 or 0 now stand up, and the team or teams of which they are members are credited with one point for each of these digits represented on the cards of those standing up. One of them goes to the blackboard and performs the operation by writing:

$$
\begin{array}{r}
345 \\
\times\,6 \\
\hline
30
\end{array}
$$

Next, the first player of the second team continues the multiplication, saying, "40 × 6 = 240." (He multiplies by 40 because the digit 4 is in the tens' position in the number 345 and signifies four tens.) Once again, all players having 2, 4, or 0 on their cards stand up and receive credit for their team. One of them writes the number 240 underneath the 30 at the blackboard, thus:

$$345$$
$$\underline{\times\ 6}$$
$$30$$
$$240$$

The multiplication is carried on by the first player of the third team, who should say, "$300 \times 6 = 1{,}800$." (He multiplies by 300 because the digit 3 stands in the hundreds' place in the number 345 and denotes three hundreds.) Now all players with the digits 1, 8, or 0 stand up. Since the digit 0 is used twice in the partial product, a bonus of five points goes to the team in which players have this digit on their cards. Again, one of the players having any of these digits goes to the blackboard and adds the partial product, 1,800, to the column, so that it looks like this:

$$345$$
$$\underline{\times\ 6}$$
$$30$$
$$240$$
$$1{,}800$$

The first player on the fourth team now goes to the blackboard, draws a line under the 1,800, adds the four columns, and enters the total, 2,070, as the product. All players with the digits 2, 0, or 7 stand up and receive one point for their respective teams for each digit represented, with a bonus of five points for the zero, since it is used twice in the answer.

Finally, the first player of the fifth team checks the answer. One of several ways of doing so is for him to divide 2,070 by 6 and derive the quotient 345.

For the next round, a new example is placed at the blackboard. This time the game starts with the second player of the fifth team, who is followed by the second player of the fourth team, and so on, down to the second player of the first team.

As indicated, one point is scored if a player gets a correct partial product—in this game, $5 \times 6 = 30$, $40 \times 6 = 240$, and $300 \times 6 = 1,800$. One point is deducted if a player gives a wrong answer. And five points are won as a bonus if the same digit is used twice in an answer.

The team first scoring a total of twenty-five points is the winner.

DIVIDE AND CONQUER

LONG DIVISION

Twenty-five or more
  players
Paper and pencil

Blackboard
Index cards

In this variation of Stand up and Be Counted, the procedure and the scoring are the same, but the examples all involve problems in long division—say, $3,995 \div 17$—instead of multiplication. To make sure that the quotients are whole numbers, the leader—parent or teacher—should first arrive at the dividends by multiplying whole numbers. Thus, in the example given above, the dividend 3,995 was derived from multiplying 17 and 235.

153

BOXING MATCH

ADDITION, SUBTRACTION, MULTIPLICATION,
DIVISION, EQUIVALENTS, FRACTIONS,
DECIMALS, ROMAN NUMERALS

Even number of ten or   Chalk
   more players   Timer
Blackboard

The only boxing that occurs in this game is the boxing in of adjacent digits on the blackboard by members of competing teams as they solve problems in arithmetic.

First, the leader—parent or teacher—writes on the blackboard the digits 0 through 9 in random order—for example, 2 3 0 1 5 9 8 6 4 7.

Next he calls out a simple arithmetic problem that has an answer consisting of digits that are adjacent in the row on the blackboard, for example, 6×5.

The first player of the first team must, within a given time limit, respond with the correct answer, which is in this case 30. He then goes to the blackboard and boxes in the adjacent 3 0, as shown in the following illustration. If he gives a wrong answer or fails to arrive at the correct answer within the time limit, his team loses two points. He scores one point for each digit that is boxed in. So in this case he would score two points.

A new problem is then called out—say 8^2. The first player of the second team must solve this problem by calling out 64 and going to the blackboard to box in the 6 and the 4, as shown here.

154

2 |3 0| 1 5 9 8 |6 4| 7

The game continues in this fashion, and more digits are circled. At any point, the numbers on the blackboard may be erased, and a new arrangement may be substituted — for example, 9 1 5 3 0 4 6 8 7.

The problems may involve addition, subtraction, multiplication, division, squares, cubes, fractions, decimals, and Roman numerals and may be graded in difficulty according to the abilities of the players. The game may also be played with equivalents: 1 quart = ____ pints; half a foot = ____ inches; half a pound = ____ ounces; 1 quarter = ____ nickels.

The team that first scores ten points wins the game.

To appreciate the possibilities of this game, consider the problems and digit combinations illustrated below, with the solutions boxed in for each one:

$9^2 =$ 3 4 9 7 2 |8 1| 5 0 6

$5 \times 5 \times 3 =$ 9 2 |7 5| 3 8 4 1 6 0

XLVIII = 1 6 5 3 2 |4 8| 0 7 9

(1/2 of 16) + (1/3 of 27) = 2 8 9 |1 7| 5 0 3 6

135 + 16 + 24 = 2 9 |1 7 5| 0 4 8 6 3

7,515 ÷ 15 = 3 |5 0 1| 6 9 8 7 4 2

$2^3 + 3^2 =$ 0 4 3 9 |1 7| 5 2 8 6

$5 \times 8 \times 7 =$ 4 9 |2 8 0| 5 3 6 1 7

3,456 − 1,292 = 9 3 |2 1 6 4| 5 8 0 7

34 × 17 = 9 2 4 3 |5 7 8| 1 6 0

155

UNBOXING MATCH

ADDITION, SUBTRACTION, MULTIPLICATION,
DIVISION, EQUIVALENTS, FRACTIONS,
DECIMALS

Even number of ten or   Chalk
  more players   Timer
Blackboard

This game is simply a reverse variation of Boxing Match.

The leader writes on the blackboard a random series of digits and boxes off two or three of them. Then, within a given time limit, each player, in turn, must "unbox" the number by making up an arithmetical problem to which the answer is in the box. For example, if the digits 2 and 5 are boxed, the answer may be 5×5 or $20 + 5$ or any other arithmetical example whose solution yields the number 25.

To make the game harder, the rules may require that the solution is to involve only division or both multiplication and addition or equivalents or fractions or decimals, depending on the abilities of the players.

In this game, one point is scored for each correct response, two points are lost to the other team if a wrong response or no response at all is given within the time limit, and a score of ten points wins.

BATTER UP!

ADDITION, SUBTRACTION, MULTIPLICATION,
DIVISION, EQUIVALENTS, FRACTIONS,
DECIMALS, ROMAN NUMERALS

Even number of ten or   Prepared cards
  more players   Timer
Blackboard

This game is played like baseball, with a diamond laid
out on the floor or at the blackboard and with a scoreboard to record hits, outs, and runs.

Prepare two sets of 3″ × 5″ cards, with thirty cards in
each set. One set — let us call it Set A — should have on
each card an easy problem in arithmetic; for example,
How many inches in half a foot? What Arabic number
corresponds to LXVI? What is the product of 3 and 9?
Set B should consist of cards containing more difficult
problems, involving combinations of multiplication or
division with addition or subtraction, fractions, decimals, etc. Keep the two sets separate.

The teams choose to see which one is up first. The members of the team that is not up take positions on the field
as pitcher, catcher, first baseman, etc. After shuffling
both sets of cards, the pitcher selects one from Set B,
with the more difficult problems, and gives it to the
member of the other team who is first at bat. Within a
given time limit, he must solve the problem. If he does
so, he advances to first base. If he does not, he is struck
out. (The leader — teacher or parent — acts as umpire.)

The first pitch was taken from the more difficult set of
problems. But if the first batter solved the problem and

advanced to first base, the second batter can choose his problem from the easier group. On the other hand, if his predecessor struck out, the second batter must be given a problem from the more difficult ones in Set B.

At any time during the game, a player in the field can challenge an opponent on base near him. For example, if a player is on second base, the second baseman can challenge him by volunteering to solve a difficult problem which he draws from Set B, like: What is the equivalent of fourscore and seven? If the challenger solves the problem, the challenged player on base is put out. If the challenger fails to solve the problem within the time limit, the player on base advances to the next base. However, a player can be challenged only once during an inning.

Keep a record of runs and outs. The team with the higher score wins after nine innings have been played, with three outs in each inning, as in baseball.

WHAT'S MY NUMBER?

DISTINGUISHING BETWEEN GREATER AND LESS
Six or more players
Besides teaching an important mathematical skill, this game places a premium on a good memory.

One player, the victim, goes out of the room while the rest agree on a number from 1 to 150.

When the victim returns, he has the task of determining what the number is by asking each player in turn a different question so phrased that it can be answered either yes or no.

Suppose, for example, that the number chosen is 15. Here is how the game might proceed:

Player 1: What's my number?
Victim: Is it greater than 100? (Question 1)
Player 1: No.
Victim: Is it greater than 50? (Question 2)
Player 2: No.
Victim: Is it less than 25? (Question 3)
Player 3: Yes.
Victim: Is it greater than 10? (Question 4)
Player 4: Yes.
Victim: Is it greater than 20? (Question 5)
Player 5: No.
Victim: Is it greater than 18? (Question 6)
Player 6: No.
Victim: Is it greater than 14? (Question 7)
Player 1: Yes.
Victim: Is it greater than 16? (Question 8)
Player 2: No.
Victim: Then your number must be 15. Is it? (Question 9)
Player 3: Yes.

Here the victim has scored nine because he needed nine questions to reach the correct answer.

Another victim and a different number are now chosen, and the game continues. The player scoring the *lowest* wins the game. If a victim cannot determine what the

number is after asking ten questions, he receives a
score of twenty, and the game continues with a new
number and a new victim.

YOUR NUMBER'S UP!

DISTINGUISHING BETWEEN
GREATER AND LESS, ODD AND EVEN;
ADDITION, SUBTRACTION, MULTIPLICATION,
DIVISION, FRACTIONS

Six or more players   Timer

This variation of What's My Number? can be used to
teach a broad range of fundamental skills in arithmetic.

Here the victim must frame each of his questions in a
form that requires the player to whom it is addressed to
perform, within a given time limit, such mathematical
operations as adding, subtracting, multiplying, dividing,
and using fractions.

Thus, the victim might ask questions like:

Is your number greater than 9×8?
Is your number less than half of 50?
Is your number divisible by 2 (that is, is it even)?
Is your number divisible by 5?
Is your number less than the sum of 30 and 15?
Is your number greater than the difference between 75
    and 20?
Is your number a prime number (that is, one not divisi-
    ble by any number other than itself and 1)?

If the player to whom a question is addressed gives the victim a wrong or misleading answer or is unable to answer within the time limit, the victim gets credit for one question fewer. Consequently, the victim will try to put his opponents on their mettle by making his questions as complicated as possible and involving the other players in a confusing set of mental operations.

SUM BINGO

ADDITION

Six or more players   Paper and pencil
Dice

Each player prepares on his paper a nine-box square and inserts in the boxes at random any numbers from 2 through 12. Below are shown the boxes of two different players.

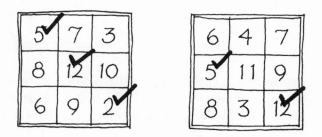

The players then take turns rolling the dice and adding the two numbers turned up. If the sum is a number in any player's box, he checks it. The game continues until one player has checked all three numbers in a column, row, or diagonal. He is the winner.

MADS BINGO

MULTIPLICATION, ADDITION, DIVISION, SUBTRACTION

Six or more players   Paper and pencil
Dice

Each player prepares on his paper a twenty-five-box square and inserts in the boxes at random the numbers 1, 2, 3, 4, 5, 6, 7, 8, 9, 10, 11, 12, 15, 16, 18, 20, 24, 25, 30, and 36, as well as 0 and again 1, 2, and 3. One box, without a number, is marked Free, as in the illustration, which shows the boxes of two different players. The Free box is always in the center.

1	15 ✓	10	24	30
16	11	0	2 ✓	20
3	8 ✓	FREE	25	12
4	1	3	36	9
18	7	5	6	2 ✓

3	1	25	16	6
15 ✓	8 ✓	7	11	5
10	12	FREE	0	3
24	4	2 ✓	1	2 ✓
30	3	9	20	36

The players take turns rolling the dice. The two numbers turned up are announced, and all the players perform on them the four operations of arithmetic (Multiplication, Addition, Division, and Subtraction) to see whether the resulting numbers match any in their boxes. They then check the boxes containing these numbers. For example, if 5 and 3 are rolled, all the players try adding them (5 + 3 = 8), subtracting the lesser from the greater (5 − 3 = 2), multiplying them (5 × 3 = 15), and dividing them (5 ÷ 3 = 1 2/3, or 2 rounded to the nearest whole number). Note that in the boxes illustrated here those containing 8, 2, and 15 have been checked.

The game proceeds in this way until one player has checked five boxes vertically, horizontally, or diagonally. If proved correct, he is the winner.

A-LOTTO-NUMBERS

ADDITION, SUBTRACTION, MULTIPLICATION, DIVISION

Six or more players   Paper and pencil
Prepared cards

First, prepare a set of twenty cards. Each card should have an example in arithmetic whose answer is one of the numbers from 1 through 20, so that every number is represented. The examples should involve addition, subtraction, multiplication, and division. Thus they might consist of the following set: $8 \div 8$, 1/2 of 10, $9 - 6$, 2×2, $250 \div 125$, $2 \times (1 + 3)$, $65 - 59$, $49 \div 7$, 1/8 of $(74 - 2)$, $5 \times (6 \div 3)$, $99 - 88$, 2/9 of 54, $(20 - 8) + 1$, $(3 + 4) \times 2$, $3 \times (95 - 90)$, $517 - 501$, $(3 \times 5) + 2$, $3 \times 2 \times 3$, $(5 \times 4) - 1$, and $500 \div 25$.

Next, each player prepares on his paper a nine-box square and inserts in the boxes at random any nine numbers from 1 through 20, as shown in the illustration on the next page.

Now shuffle the cards and place them facedown on the table. Turn over the top card and let every player see

7	3	8
6	9	15
4	16	10

the example on it. Each player quietly tries to solve the problem, and, if the answer is a number in a box on his paper, he checks it.

Continue in this way until one player has checked every number on his card. Before he is declared a winner, be sure to verify his answers.

In later rounds larger numbers and more difficult problems may be used, and the square may be expanded to twenty-five boxes.

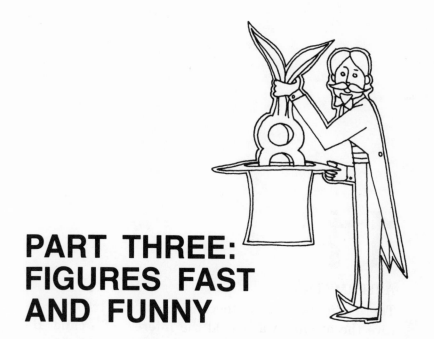

PART THREE: FIGURES FAST AND FUNNY

11

ARITHMETRICKS

There is nothing like a touch of magic or a trick to capture the attention and hold the interest of a child. He derives a real sense of power from mystifying his friends by performing such occult feats as reading their minds, using extrasensory perception, or instantly solving apparently difficult problems. With the "mathemagical" tricks in this chapter, any child can soon become a "whizzard" with numbers!

SUM SPEED

Just to show how fast you can add, you invite a friend to write down two four-digit numbers. Seeming to help him, you write a third four-digit number under his two, draw a line, and instantly put down their sum. To his surprise, your instantaneous addition proves correct. What's more, you repeat this feat of fast figuring with him as many times as he likes, with whatever two four-digit numbers he selects.

The secret is that the digits of your third number consist of the difference, in each case, between 9 and the corresponding digits of his second number, and your total begins with the digit 1, follows with the first three digits of his first number, and ends with a digit that is one less than the value of the last digit in his first number.

Let's see how this would work if he selects: 2,653
                                              4,723

You write the difference between 9,999 and
  4,723:   5,276
And immediately give the total: 12,652

Note that the number you added, 5,276, when added to his second number, 4,723, produces a total of 9,999. Note also that the final total, 12,652, consists of a 1 followed by the first three digits of his first number and the digit 2, which is one less than the value of the last digit (3) in his first number, 2,653.

Let's try this again with a different set: 7,891
                                             5,306
You insert 9,999 − 5,306 =   4,693
And immediately write the total: 17,890

SUM MYSTERY

This is a good trick to baffle a friend with.

Just tell him to write down any three four-digit numbers in a column. As soon as he has done so, you quickly write under his numbers three more four-digit numbers, draw a line under the entire column, and immediately write their sum—29,997. He checks the addition, and you are right! How could you have added the column so fast? Or how could you have known what numbers to write in so quickly in order to arrive at that sum?

It is easy once you know the trick. The numbers you added *had* to equal 29,997 when added to his numbers, no matter what his numbers were. How so? Because you made sure, in writing your numbers, to put down digits that, in every instance, when added to the corresponding digits in his numbers, would total nine. Thus you made three sums of 9,999 or 9,999 × 3, which equal 29,997.

For example, suppose he writes:	4,651
	7,218
	3,912
Then you immediately add the numbers:	5,348
	2,781
	6,087
And sum it all up at once as:	29,997

Note that 4,651 (his first number) and 5,348 (your first number) add up to 9,999. Similarly, 7,218 + 2,781 = 3,912 + 6,087 = 9,999. Small wonder, then, that the sum is what it is.

If three-digit numbers are used, the total will be 2,997, which is 999 × 3.

Thus, if you friend writes:	582
	275
	316
You just add:	417
	724
	683
And immediately write down the sum:	2,997

The game can be played with five-digit numbers, six-digit numbers, or even larger ones. To determine the sum in each case, write side by side as many 9s as there are digits in the number less one, and then place a 2 as the first digit and a 7 as the last. For example, the sum when the trick is played with five-place numbers is 29,9997, that is, *four* 9s (one fewer than the number of digits) between the 2 and the 7.

You can, if you wish, write your numbers alternately with your friend's; the result will be the same.

Of course, the larger the numbers you begin with, the more mystifying the trick becomes. But do not play it too often with the same friend!

If you play this trick with four three-digit numbers for your friend and four for yourself, the sum will be 999 × 4 = 3,996; with four four-digit numbers each, 39,996; etc. A really dazzling feat is to play the trick with five four-digit numbers, making ten large numbers to add in a jiffy. 9,999 × 5 = 49,995. From here on, you can continue to escalate as you like.

PSYCHIC ARITHMETIC

You can tell what number your friend is thinking of!

But first he has to write down any three-digit number without telling you what it is.

Then he must write under it the same number with the digits in reverse order. (If the original number ends in zero, his reverse number must begin with a zero.)

Next he subtracts the reversed number from the original number.

Finally he must reverse the remainder and add this reversed number to the remainder.

You tell him to concentrate hard on the resulting number. After a moment of silence, you announce, to his utter amazement, the exact number he was thinking of. You ask to see his paper. Yes, you were right!

How did you do it?

You couldn't miss, unless he made a mistake in arithmetic. The number had to be 1,089.

Try it and see.

Suppose he starts with:	572
He then reverses this number:	275
Subtracting, he gets:	297
Now, reversing the remainder, he writes:	792
And adding, he cannot help but arrive at:	1,089

Or suppose he started with:	790
Then he reversed and wrote:	097
The remainder is:	693
Reversed, this is:	396
And the sum is again:	1,089

If subtraction involves taking a larger number from a smaller, just tell your friend to interchange the sub-trahend and the minuend and to subtract as usual.

So if he starts with:	249
And he reverses to get:	942
Just tell him to interchange and subtract:	942
	249
To get the remainder:	693
And then reverse:	396
To come out with the predictable sum:	1,089

You can't miss! But again, it is best not to play this trick on the same friend more than once.

ODDS AND EVENS

Tell your friend to hold an odd number of coins or pebbles in one hand and an even number in the other. Let him do this without your seeing which hand holds the odd number and which holds the even.

Now ask him to multiply the number in his right hand by two and the number in his left hand by three. Then have him add the two products and tell you their sum.

Immediately you tell him which hand has the odd number of items and which hand has the even number. You ask him to open his hands, and you are, of course, right as usual. You try it again, and again you are right. No matter how many times you try it, you are always able to tell him where the odd number is and where the even number is.

How do you know?

If the sum is odd, the left hand holds the odd number; if the sum is even, the left hand holds the even number. That is all there is to it! Try it and see for yourself.

ODD OR EVEN?

Give a friend a pack of cards and ask him to remove a number of them and count them secretly to see whether he has an odd or an even number of cards. After he has done this, take a few cards from the pack yourself. Then tell your friend that when your cards are added to his, the total number of cards will be an even number if he has an odd number of cards, or an odd number if he is holding an even number of cards. To his astonishment you prove to be right.

It is easy when you know the trick. Always take an odd number of cards from the pack—three, five, seven, etc. If you add these to an odd number—say, five—the total will be an even number—eight, ten, twelve, etc. If you add an odd number to an even number—say, four—the total will always be an odd number—seven, nine, eleven, etc.

DIVISION PRECISION

Ask your friend to draw any two cards from a pack and show them to you. (If you try this trick with two friends, you can have each one draw a card.) All you ask is the right to pick any card you like from the rest of the deck, and you will guarantee, in a jiffy, to use the three cards to make a number that can be divided evenly by eleven without leaving any remainder.

Suppose the two cards drawn are a 3 and a 5. Just draw from the pack either the difference between 3 and 5— that is, any 2 in the deck—or the sum of 3 and 5—that is, any 8. Now all you do is arrange the three cards quickly so that the card in the middle has a number equal to the sum of the numbers on the other two cards. For example, with 2, 3, and 5, arrange the cards to make 253; with 3, 5, and 8, arrange the cards to make 385. In either case, the result is precisely divisible by eleven. You can make this trick even more mystifying by having your friend pick just one card from the pack, to be matched by two selected by you in less than half a minute. Then, if he picks a 7, for instance, you just pick any other card—say, 8—and immediately thereafter find a third card with a number that represents the difference between the larger number and the smaller: $8 - 7 = 1$. Since an ace has the value of 1, place the 8, the sum of 7 and 1, between these numbers, and the result will be 781, a number perfectly divisible by eleven.

THE CASE OF THE MISSING NUMBER

You tell your friend that you are a detective who can trace missing numbers. Does he know of a missing number? You will find it quickly.

Ask him to write down any string of numbers, without showing you the result. Say he writes: 714,329,167
Next, have him add a zero to the right: 7,143,291,670
Now let him subtract his first number: 714,329,167
Ask him to write down the remainder: 6,428,962,503
Finally, tell him to eliminate any digit except zero from the number he has left. Say he eliminates the 4. Then his remaining number will be: 628,962,503

You now state that if he will show you just his remaining number, you will tell him what number he eliminated — that is, you will find the missing number.

Here is how you do it. First, add the digits in the remaining number he gives you. In this case, $6 + 2 + 8 + 9 + 6 + 2 + 5 + 0 + 3 =$ 41

Then add the digits in the remaining number: $4 + 1 = 5$ (If the sum still contains more than one digit, keep on adding the digits until you end with a number consisting of only one digit.)

The single-digit number you finally get, if it is 9, is the missing number. If the single-digit number you end with is any number but 9, subtract it from 9 to find the missing number. In this case, $9 - 5 = 4$, the missing number.

THE EXACT CARD

Tell your friend that, with only the aid of a little arithmetic on his part, you will detect, with perfect exactness, not only the numerical value but the suit of any card he draws from a deck.

Let him shuffle the cards himself. When he has drawn his card, have him double its numerical value, add one to the result, and multiply this sum by five. If the card is a club, he is now to add six; if a heart, seven; if a spade, eight; and if a diamond, nine. You now ask him for the number he has ended with, and, as soon as he tells you, you inform him of the exact numerical value and the suit of the card he drew.

Don't worry. You can do this every time. What's more, you will leave him completely mystified each time you do it.

If the number he ends with consists of two digits, all you do is subtract one from the tens' digit. This will give you the numerical value of the card he has drawn. The number in the units' digit corresponds to the position of the initial letter of the name of the suit in the word "chased," if you disregard the letters "a" and "e": if it is 1, then the card he drew is a club; if the units' digit is 2, the card he drew is a heart; if the digit is 3, his card is a spade; and if the digit is 4, his card is a diamond.

For example, if he drew a 5 of clubs, he doubled the 5 to get $5 \times 2 = 10$, to which he added 1: $10 + 1 = 11$. This he multiplied by 5: $11 \times 5 = 55$. And to this he added 6 because his card was a club: $55 + 6 = 61$. Subtracting 1 from the tens' digit (6), you get $6 - 1 = 5$, the numerical value of the card he drew. The 1 in the units' position in the number 61 corresponds to the position of the "c" in the word "chased" and reveals to you that his card was a club.

If your friend ends with a three-digit number, this means that you subtract 1 from the number formed by the hundreds' digit and the tens' digit. This will give you the numerical value of the card he has drawn. Once again, the units' digit will indicate the suit.

For example, if he drew the king of hearts, he multiplied 13 (the value assigned to a king) by 2: $13 \times 2 = 26$. To this he added 1: $26 + 1 = 27$. Then he multiplied by 5: $27 \times 5 = 135$. Adding 7 to this number (because he drew a card from the hearts' suit) gives him: $135 + 7 = 142$. The 2 in the units' place tells you that he has drawn a heart, since "h" is the second letter in the word "chased." The 14 in the number 142 is then reduced by 1: $14 - 1 = 13$. This tells you that he drew a king.

A jack is valued at 11; a queen, at 12.

This trick always works if you and your friend both do your arithmetic right.

THE PRECISE WORD

This trick depends on an oddity of arithmetic. If you multiply a number by one hundred, subtract the original number, and then add the digits in the remainder, their sum will always be eighteen.

For example, take 8. Multiply by 100: $8 \times 100 = 800$. Now subtract the original number: $800 - 8 = 792$. If you add the digits in 792, you get $7 + 9 + 2 = 18$.

No matter what number you start with, the result will always be the same.

You can make use of this knowledge to mystify your friends. Present yourself as a "whizz-ard" who can predict the precise word to be found at the beginning of a page in a book. (You make sure, of course, in advance, when no one is looking, to find out just what word does appear as the first word on page 18 of the particular book you intend to use for this trick.) When your friend has chosen his number and has gone through all the arithmetical operations that you ask him to carry out, he will naturally tell you that his number is 18. Ask him to pick up the book and turn to page 18. He is to concentrate hard on the word that appears first on that page. Then you tell him, to his amazement, the precise word.

If you have two books before you and have memorized the first word on page 18 of each, you can let your friend choose the book he wants to test you with.

Having played this trick once, you should use a different procedure the next time you try it with the same friend. This time have him add to his original number the next higher number, add 9 to this sum, and divide the result by 2. Let him now subtract the original number. The answer will always be 5. You proceed in the same way, except that you memorize the first word on the fifth page of the book you are using.

For example, if your friend starts with 27, he adds to it the next higher number, 28: $28 + 27 = 55$. To this he adds 9: $55 + 9 = 64$. This he divides by 2: $64 \div 2 = 32$. And from the result he subtracts his original number, 27: $32 - 27 = 5$.

Another variation of this trick is also possible. Ask your friend to take any three-digit number having repeated digits. Let him divide the number by the sum of the digits. The result will always be 37. So you can tell him the first word on page 37 of the book you are using if you have prepared yourself by memorizing it.

Thus, if your friend chooses 444 and if he divides this by the sum of the digits, that is, by $4 + 4 + 4 = 12$, then the result will be $444 \div 12 = 37$. If he chooses 333, and if he divides this by the sum of the digits, that is, by $3 + 3 + 3 = 9$, the result will be $333 \div 9 = 37$.

WHAT ARE THE ODDS?

Take five cards or slips of paper. Write the number 1 on one side of one of the cards and a 2 on the back; on the next card write a 3 on the front and a 4 on the back. Proceed in this way consecutively through the fifth card, with a 9 on the front and a 10 on the back, so that each card has an odd number on one side and the following even number on the other.

Now shuffle the cards and hand them to a friend. Turn your back and tell him to let the cards fall on the table haphazardly. If he tells you how many cards with odd numbers are facing up, you will instantly tell him the sum of the numbers on all the cards turned up. You do this every time he tries with a different combination of numbers.

Mystifying as this trick is, it depends on a very simple fact: the sum of the even numbers from 2 through $10 = 30 = 2 + 4 + 6 + 8 + 10$. Hence, all you have to do is to subtract from 30 the number of odd cards turned up. The difference will equal the total of the numbers on all the cards that are faceup.

For example, suppose he puts down 2, 3, 5, 8, and 10. He tells you that there are two odd cards in this group. $30 - 2 = 28 = 2 + 3 + 5 + 8 + 10$.

If you use six cards, going up to 12, the total of the even numbers is 42. Subtract from this number the number of odd cards to determine the sum of the numbers on all the cards turned up. Thus, if the cards turned up are 6, 8, 9, 1, 11, and 3, and you are told that the group includes four odd cards, then the total $= 42 - 4 = 38 = 6 + 8 + 9 + 1 + 11 + 3$.

Once you understand the principle, you can apply it to any number of similarly prepared cards.

ADDITION MAGICIAN

Invite three of your friends to observe you demonstrate that you are an addition magician.

Take nine cards from a deck from which you have eliminated all tens, jacks, queens, and kings. Divide the cards into three sets of three cards each. Privately note the totals of the numbers in each set. Suppose, for example, that one set consists of 6, 7, and 8; another, of 5, 9, and 2; and the third, of 3, 7, and 5. The total of the first set is 21; of the second set, 16; and of the third set, 15. On a slip of paper, write these totals down in this form:

$$
\begin{array}{r}
21 \\
16 \\
+ \quad 15 \\
\hline
\end{array}
$$

Add them: 2275

Put the nine cards back on top of the deck, in the exact order of the three sets. Have the first friend, A, take the top three cards; the second friend, B, draw the next three; and the third friend, C, take the last three. Ask them to shuffle their cards. A now turns up any one of his cards — say, 7. You now say that the total of the three three-digit numbers they will produce will equal 2,275. B next gives you any one of his three cards — say, 2. You write on a paper: 72. C gives you, let us say, his 3. Your number becomes: 723. On the second round, A may give you his 8; B, his 5; and C, his 7. You write 857. On the third round, A gives you his last card, 6; B, 9; and C, 5. You write 695. Now, 723 + 857 + 695 = 2,275.

No matter how many times you try this trick, you will always be able to predict the total, no matter in what order your friends turn up their cards, if you follow the procedure above.

12

SHORTCUTS IN ARITHMETIC

Finding a shortcut in arithmetic is like finding a shortcut to success. Nothing gives a child a greater feeling of confidence in his intellectual powers than to be able to multiply and divide big numbers with the utmost ease and accuracy and to check in an instant the addition of several long columns of figures.

These shortcuts are not games, nor are they the "easy way out," but rather the quick and efficient way to the correct performance of otherwise difficult and time-consuming computations.

MULTIPLICATION BY TEN

One of the simplest shortcuts is useful in multiplying by ten. Just add a zero after the last digit of the number being multiplied.

Thus, $72 \times 10 = 720$. And $720 \times 10 = 7,200$.

If multiplying decimals by ten, simply move the decimal point one place to the right.

For example, $169.3 \times 10 = 1,693$. And $169.35 \times 10 = 1,693.5$.

MULTIPLICATION BY FIVE

The same principle can be applied in quickly multiplying by five, since five is half of ten.

To multiply by five, first multiply by ten, and then divide by two.

For example, $39 \times 5 = \dfrac{39 \times 10}{2} = 390 \div 2 = 195$.

Applying this rule to decimals, move the decimal point one place to the right, and then divide by two.

Thus, $186.4 \times 5 = \dfrac{186.4 \times 10}{2} = 1,864 \div 2 = 932$.

MULTIPLICATION BY FIFTEEN

Now that you know how to multiply quickly by ten and by five, you can also speed multiplication by their sum, fifteen.

Just add the totals resulting from multiplication by ten and multiplication by five.

Example 1: $635 \times 15 = (635 \times 10) + \dfrac{635 \times 10}{2} = 6{,}350 +$

$\dfrac{6{,}350}{2} = 6{,}350 + 3{,}175 = 9{,}525.$

Example 2: $4{,}582.6 \times 15 = (4{,}582.6 \times 10) + \dfrac{4{,}582.6 \times 10}{2} =$

$45{,}826 + \dfrac{45{,}826}{2} = 45{,}826 + 22{,}913 = 68{,}739.$

MULTIPLICATION BY NINE

Multiplying by nine is like multiplying by ten minus one.

First multiply by ten, and then subtract the original number from the product.

Example 1: $216 \times 9 = (216 \times 10) - 216 = 2{,}160 - 216 = 1{,}944.$

Example 2: $63.4 \times 9 = (63.4 \times 10) - 63.4 = 634 - 63.4 = 570.6.$

MULTIPLICATION BY ONE HUNDRED

Since one hundred is ten times ten, just add two zeroes when multiplying by one hundred.

Thus, $5 \times 100 = 500.$ And $35 \times 100 = 3{,}500.$

If multiplying decimals, move the decimal point two places to the right.

For example, $5.2 \times 100 = 5.20 \times 100 = 520$.

MULTIPLICATION BY ONE THOUSAND

As one thousand is ten times one hundred, merely add three zeroes when multiplying by one thousand.

For instance, $9 \times 1,000 = 9,000$. And $19 \times 1,000 = 19,000$.

If multiplying decimals, move the decimal point three places to the right.

Thus, $7.8 \times 1,000 = 7.800 \times 1,000 = 7,800$.

MULTIPLICATION BY ELEVEN

This is most easily accomplished if the number to be multiplied consists of just two digits.

In that case, simply add the digits and write their sum between them.

Thus, to multiply 35 by 11, first add the digits 3 and 5. $3 + 5 = 8$. Now place the 8 between the 3 and the 5. The result is 385.

DIVISIBILITY

It is often helpful to know in advance what numbers can be divided exactly into a given number. For example, can 59,346 be exactly divided by 3? Can 781,253 be divided exactly by 9? The answer to both of these questions is yes. But how do you know?

There are a number of simple rules—tricks, if you wish to call them so—that can serve as shortcuts. If you learn them, you will save much time and energy. Here they are.

DIVISIBILITY BY TWO

If the given number ends in an even digit or in zero, it is divisible by two.

For example, 1,634 is divisible by two because the last digit is 4, an even number. So is 61,830 divisible by two, because the last digit is zero.

DIVISIBILITY BY THREE

For a number to be divisible by three, the sum of its digits must be divisible by three.

Thus the sum of the digits in 59,346 is $5 + 9 + 3 + 4 + 6 = 27$, a number divisible by three. Therefore, 59,346 is exactly divisible by three.

DIVISIBILITY
BY FOUR

A number is divisible by four if its last two digits, taken by themselves, form a number that is divisible by four.

For example, the last two digits of 534,924 are 24, which is divisible by four. Therefore, so is 534,924.

DIVISIBILITY
BY FIVE

If the last digit of a number is a five or a zero, the number is exactly divisible by five.

Accordingly, in 3,417,825, the last digit is 5; so the whole number is exactly divisible by five. The same is true of 713,980 because the last digit is zero.

DIVISIBILITY
BY SIX

If a number is divisible by three and also divisible by two, it will be divisible by their product, six.

Take, for instance, the number 24,312. $2 + 4 + 3 + 1 + 2 = 12$, which is divisible by three; hence, the number is divisible by three. As the last digit (2) is even, the number is also divisible by two. Therefore, 24,312 is divisible by six.

DIVISIBILITY BY EIGHT

If the last three digits of a number, taken by themselves, form a number that is divisible by eight, then so is the original number.

Thus, in the number 417,344, the last three digits, taken by themselves, form the number 344. $344 \div 8 = 43$. So 417,344 is also divisible by eight.

DIVISIBILITY BY NINE

If the sum of the digits of a number is divisible by nine, then the original number is also divisible by nine.

For example, the sum of the digits in 7,314,831 is $7 + 3 + 1 + 4 + 8 + 3 + 1 = 27$. Since 27 is divisible by nine, so is 7,314,831.

DIVISIBILITY BY TEN

Any number having zero as its last digit is divisible by ten.

For example, since 35,780 has zero as its last digit, it is divisible by ten.

DIVISIBILITY BY TWELVE

First see whether the number is divisible by three. Then determine whether it is also divisible by four. If it is divisible by both three and four, it must be divisible by their product, which is twelve.

Take, for example, the number 9,324:

9 + 3 + 2 + 4 = 18, a number divisible by three. So 9,324 is also divisible by three.

The last two digits of 9,324, taken by themselves, make the number 24, which is divisible by four. So 9,324 is likewise divisible by four.

Therefore, 9,324 is divisible by twelve.

CHECKING THE RESULTS OF COMPUTATIONS

There are several quick ways of checking the results of addition, subtraction, multiplication, and division without actually doing all your arithmetic over again.

One common method is called "casting out nines." You first add the digits in each of the numbers that appear in your addition, subtraction, or multiplication problem. (Division problems will be discussed separately.) Then, if necessary, add the digits of each sum until you end, in each case, with a single digit. For example, suppose you have the following addition problem:

$573 + 692 + 834 = 2{,}099.$

We obtain the following sums from the digits in this problem:

$$5 + 7 + 3 = 15$$
$$6 + 9 + 2 = 17$$
$$8 + 3 + 4 = 15.$$

Since these sums are not single digits, we must add the digits in each sum.

$$1 + 5 = 6$$
$$1 + 7 = 8$$
$$1 + 5 = 6.$$

These single digits are next added, or subtracted, or multiplied (according to the operation being checked), and the resulting number is treated in the same way as just described; that is, its digits are added until only one digit is left. The problem we are checking in this example is an addition problem.

$$6 + 8 + 6 = 20$$
$$2 + 0 = \mathbf{2.}$$

Now do the same with the answer you arrived at as a result of your original computation. In this example

$$2 + 0 + 9 + 9 = 20$$
$$2 + 0 = \mathbf{2.}$$

The digit you have left, in this case 2, is the same as the digit you have left in the previous operation; this means you obtained the right answer to your original problem (and that you most likely arrived at the answer by correctly performing the operations in your original computation, though there are rare cases when errors in computation cancel each other out).

Let's apply the same procedure to check a subtraction.

$9,342 - 8,576 = 766.$
$7 + 6 + 6 = 19. 1 + 9 = 10. 1 + 0 = 1.$
$9 + 3 + 4 + 2 = 18. 8 + 1 = 9.$
$8 + 5 + 7 + 6 = 26. 2 + 6 = 8.$
$9 - 8 = 1.$

We can do the same to verify a multiplication.

$358 \times 24 = 8,592.$
$8 + 5 + 9 + 2 = 24. 2 + 4 = 6.$
$3 + 5 + 8 = 16. 1 + 6 = 7.$
$2 + 4 = 6.$
$7 \times 6 = 42.$
$4 + 2 = 6.$

To check a division, multiply the quotient by the divisor, provided that there is no remainder in the quotient. The product should be the dividend. You can doublecheck by verifying the multiplication by the method of casting out nines.

$10,800 \div 25 = 432.$
$432 \times 25 = 10,800. 1 + 8 + 0 + 0 = 9.$
$4 + 3 + 2 = 9.$

$$2 + 5 = 7.$$
$$9 \times 7 = 63.$$
$$6 + 3 = 9.$$

If as a result of casting out nines, the final digits are not equal, then the addition, subtraction, multiplication, or division is wrong and should be done over again. If the final digits are equal, you know that the original answer is the right one and that your computation was probably correct.

ADDING NUMBERS IN A SERIES

Numbers are in a series when each one differs from the next by the same amount. For example, in the series 7, 8, 9, 10, each number differs from the next by one; in the series 3, 5, 7, 9, 11, each number differs from its neighbor by two.

Here is a shortcut for adding numbers in a series.

First, count the number of terms in the series. If the number of terms in the series is odd, take the middle number and multiply it by the number of terms in the series. The result will be their sum.

For instance, in the series 7, 8, 9, 10, 11, there are five terms in the series. Multiply the middle number, 9, by 5: $9 \times 5 = 45$. That is precisely the sum of the numbers in the series: $7 + 8 + 9 + 10 + 11 = 45$.

Again, in the series 5, 8, 11, 14, and 17, take the middle number, 11, and multiply it by the number of terms in the series, 5. $11 \times 5 = 55$. Check the result. $5 + 8 + 11 + 14 + 17 = 55$.

But if the number of terms in the series is even, you must follow a different procedure. Take the average of the two middle numbers by adding them and dividing by two. Multiply this by the number of terms in the series, and you have the sum of all the numbers in the series.

Let's try this shortcut with the series 3, 5, 7, 9. The two middle numbers are 5 and 7. Their average is $6 = (5 + 7) \div 2 = 12 \div 2$. There are four terms in the series. $6 \times 4 = 24 = 3 + 5 + 7 + 9$.

SHORTCUTS WITH FRACTIONS

The *long* way of adding or subtracting fractions is to find the common denominator first and then add or subtract. For example, if you want to add 1/2 and 1/3, you must first convert 1/2 to 3/6 and then convert 1/3 to 2/6 before adding the numerators to get their sum, 5/6.

A *short* way of getting the same result is to follow the arrows as illustrated here: $\frac{1}{2} \diagup\!\!\!\!\diagdown \frac{1}{3}$. You then get $\frac{3(1) + 2(1)}{2 \times 3} = \frac{3 + 2}{6} = \frac{5}{6}$. Let's try this procedure with $\frac{3}{8} + \frac{1}{7}$. This converts to $\frac{7(3) + 8(1)}{7 \times 8} = \frac{21 + 8}{56} = \frac{29}{56}$.

Mixed numbers should be changed to fractions first. $1\,1/2 + 1/3 = \frac{3}{2} \diagup\!\!\!\!\diagdown \frac{1}{3} = \frac{3(3) + 2(1)}{6} = \frac{9 + 2}{6} = \frac{11}{6} = 1\,5/6$.

You follow the same procedure in subtracting fractions.

$$\frac{5}{8} \diagup\!\!\!\!\diagdown \frac{1}{2} = \frac{5(2) - 8(1)}{8 \times 2} = \frac{10 - 8}{16} = \frac{2}{16} = 1/8.$$

Here is how you would subtract with a mixed number:

$$1\ 1/2 - 2/3 = \frac{3}{2} \diagup\!\!\!\!\diagdown \frac{2}{3} = \frac{3(3) - 2(2)}{2 \times 3} = \frac{9 - 4}{6} = 5/6.$$

MULTIPLICATION OF CERTAIN TYPES OF NUMBERS

There are certain types of numbers that you can multiply very quickly provided you can identify them and you know the rule.

You should be able to solve instantly such problems in multiplication as the following: 69×61, 67×63, 88×82, 73×77, 104×106, 212×218.

Did you notice what all these problems have in common? If they involve two-digit numbers, the digits on the left (the tens' digits) of both the multiplicand and the multiplier are the same, and the digits on the right (the units' digits) of both numbers add up to ten. Thus, in 69×61, $6 = 6$, and $9 + 1 = 10$. If the numbers to be multiplied contain three digits, then the first two digits on the left are the same in both numbers, and the units' digits add up to ten.

All you do is add one to the tens' digit in a two-digit number or to the number formed by the two left-hand digits in a three-digit number, multiply the sum by the other tens' digit or by the number formed by the two left-hand digits in a three-digit number, and multiply the two units' digits. Join the two products to form a number that will equal the product of the two original numbers.

Let's follow this procedure step by step with 65×65.

First, add one to the tens' digit: $6 + 1 = 7$.

Next, multiply the sum by the other tens' digit: $7 \times 6 = 42$.

Then, multiply the two units' digits: $5 \times 5 = 25$.

Finally, set the two products side by side to form the answer: 4,225. $4,225 = 65 \times 65$.

The same procedure can be followed in multiplying 86 by 84.

$8 + 1 = 9$. $9 \times 8 = 72$. $6 \times 4 = 24$. $7,224 = 86 \times 84$.

13

ODDITIES OF ARITHMETIC

The realm of numbers is full of fascinating oddities. A child's interest in arithmetic can often be awakened or sustained by an awareness of the wealth of surprises and entertaining novelties that an exploration of its byways will reveal.

Familiarity with the intriguing peculiarities of arithmetic featured in this chapter can inspire a youngster with a sense of the wonder of mathematics. At the same time, he will be able to share his new knowledge and excitement with his friends, as well as challenge them intellectually, awe them and outwit them with his easy solution of apparently baffling and even intricate problems, and show them that he knows something they do not. In fact, he will be impelled to seek for more examples like these to add to his powers and increase both his love of mathematics and his ability in it.

These odd problems are not merely riddles with a fun ending; they can be solved! They give a child practice in mathematical thinking.

■ Write 2 using seven 2s.

$$2 + \frac{22}{22} - \frac{2}{2} = 2.$$

■ What three figures multiplied by 4 will make 5?
1.25.

■ Can you use just eight 8s to get a total of 1,000?
$8 + 8 + 8 + 88 + 888 = 1000.$

■ Can you add four 2s together to get a total of 5?

$$2 + 2 + \frac{2}{2} = 5.$$

■ Can you add four 9s together to get a total of 20?
$9 + 99/9 = 20.$

■ What three digits give the same result whether they are added or multiplied?
1, 2, and 3. $1 + 2 + 3 = 1 \times 2 \times 3 = 6.$

■ Can you make five identical digits equal 100?
$111 - 11 = (33 \times 3) + 3/3 = (5 \times 5 \times 5) - (5 \times 5) = (5 + 5 + 5 + 5) \times 5 = 100.$

■ Write quickly eleven thousand eleven hundred and eleven.
12,111.

■ Arrange the figures 1, 2, 3, 4, 5, 6, 7, 8, and 9 so that their sum will be 100.
There are three different ways of solving the problem:
$15 + 36 + 47 = 98 + 2 = 100.$
$56 + 8 + 4 + 3 = 71 + 29 = 100.$
$95 \ 1/2 + 4 \ 38/76 = 100.$

■ What two-digit number is twice the product of its digits?
$36 = 2 \times (6 \times 3) = 2 \times 18$.

■ Using the same number three times, express the number 13.
There are two ways of doing this:
$12 + 12/12 = 14 - 14/14 = 13$.

■ Using the same number four times, express the number 17.
There are two ways of doing this:
$8 + 8 + 8/8 = 9 + 9 - 9/9 = 17$.

■ Using the same number five times, express the number 19.
There are two ways of doing this:
$$18 + \frac{(18 + 18)}{(18 + 18)} = 20 - \frac{(20 + 20)}{(20 + 20)} = 19.$$

■ What number, when multiplied by itself, is less than when divided by itself?
Any proper fraction. For example: $\frac{1/4}{1/4} = 1. \left(\frac{1}{4} \times \frac{1}{4} = \frac{1}{16}\right)$

■ Write down five odd digits that will add up to 14.
$11 + 1 + 1 + 1 = 14$.

■ Can you write an even number, using only odd digits?
There are many, such as 5 5/5, 7 7/7, etc.

■ Arrange the figures 1, 2, 3, 4, 5, 6, 7, 8, and 9 in two groups of four figures each so that the sum of one group will be equal to the sum of the other group.
$4 + 173 = 85 + 92 = 177$.

■ Can you add the numbers 1, 2, 3, 4, 5, 6, and 7, arranged in sequence, and total 100?
$1 + 2 + 34 + 56 + 7 = 100$.

■ Which is greater, six dozen dozen or a half a dozen dozen?
Six dozen dozen = $6 \times 12 \times 12 = 864$, whereas a half a dozen dozen = $\frac{1}{2} \times (12 \times 12) = 72$.

■ A frog is at the bottom of a thirty-foot well. If he climbs three feet and slips back two feet every hour, how many hours will it take him to get out of the well?
Twenty-eight hours. At the end of the twenty-seventh hour the frog will have reached a height of twenty-seven feet, or just three feet short of the top. During the twenty-eighth hour he will climb these last three feet and be out of the well.

■ An amoeba divides and doubles each second. In two seconds, there are four; in the third second, there are eight; etc. If it takes sixty seconds to fill a test tube with amoebae, how long will it take them to fill half the test tube?
Fifty-nine seconds. In the sixtieth second, the number of amoebae filling half the test tube will double and fill the whole test tube.

■ A man paid one dollar for having a board sawed into two sections. How much should he pay for having it sawed into four sections?
Three dollars. Dividing the board into two sections required one cutting operation, costing one dollar. Dividing each of these two sections in two, to make four sections in all, would take two more cutting operations, at one dollar each.

■ If six cats eat six rats in six minutes, how many cats will it take to eat a hundred rats in a hundred minutes at the same rate?

Since these six cats eat one rat every minute, only these six cats will be needed to eat a hundred rats in a hundred minutes.

■ How long would it take you to cut up thirty yards of cloth into one-yard lengths if you cut off one yard each day?

Twenty-nine days. At the end of the twenty-eighth day, you would have cut twenty-eight one-yard lengths and would have left a piece of cloth two yards in length. On the twenty-ninth day, by snipping this two-yard length in half, you would have cut off one yard more and have an additional yard left over, making thirty one-yard lengths in all.

■ Can you write the numbers 1 through 9 in the circles so that the four lines of three figures total 69?

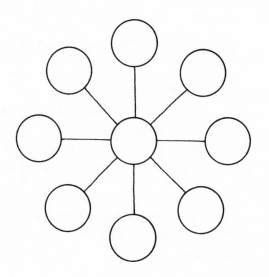

Here is the answer:

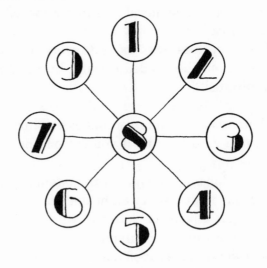

■ Is there any difference between a piece of property covering a square mile and another that is a mile square? There is no difference in area, but there could be a difference in shape. A mile square is a square consisting of four sides each of which is a mile long. A square mile can be of any shape.

■ A farmer had twenty sheep. All but eleven died. How many did he have left?
Eleven.

■ What is the difference between twenty four-quart bottles and twenty-four quart bottles?
Fifty-six quarts. Twenty four-quart bottles hold eighty quarts. Twenty-four quart bottles hold twenty-four quarts.

■ A boy went to a spring with a five-quart can and a three-quart can to fetch exactly four quarts of water. How did he measure it?

■ Can you arrange the digits from 1 through 9 on the three sides of a triangle so that the sum of the digits on each side will be 17?

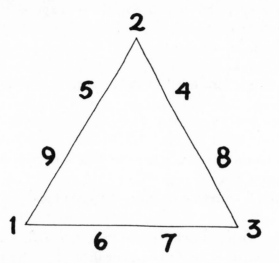

■ Arrange three 9s to get 9.
There are two ways of doing this:
$9 + 9 - 9 = 9 (9/9) = 9$.

■ Arrange three 9s to get 11.
$$\frac{99}{9} = 11.$$

■ Arrange the digits from 1 through 9 in two rows whose sums are equal.

■ What four different odd numbers add up to 20?
$1 + 3 + 7 + 9 = 20$.

■ Using only the digit 3 five times, express the number 31.
$3^3 + 3 + 3/3 = 31$.

■ What integer added to itself is greater than (>) its square?
1. $1 + 1 = 2$. $1 \times 1 = 1$. $2 > 1$.

■ With what four weights can you weigh any number of pounds from 1 to 15?
1 pound, 2 pounds, 4 pounds, and 8 pounds.

■ Using each of the ten digits 0, 1, 2, 3, 4, 5, 6, 7, 8, and 9 only once, express the number 0.
$1 \times 2 \times 3 \times 4 \times 5 \times 6 \times 7 \times 8 \times 9 \times 0 = 0$.

■ Can you express the number 100 as a mixed number using all the digits from 1 through 9 only once and with only one figure in the integral part of the number? (See Appendix for definitions of these terms.)
$3 + \dfrac{69{,}258}{714} = 100$.

■ Even though you reverse the order of the digits in the following sum, the total will be the same:
$98 + 87 + 69 + 49 + 22 + 54 + 67 + 76 + 83 = 605$.
See for yourself: $89 + 78 + 96 + 94 + 22 + 45 + 76 + 67 + 38 = 605$.

■ Multiply 99 by any number from 1 to 100, and the product will always be a number whose digits total 18.

See for yourself: $99 \times 5 = 495$. $4 + 9 + 5 = 18$. $99 \times 72 = 7,128$. $7 + 1 + 2 + 8 = 18$.

■ What number other than zero, when added to itself, gives the same result as when multiplied by itself?
2. $2 + 2 = 2 \times 2 = 4$.

■ Here are five sets of two figures each, which, when added together, result in every instance in a sum whose digits are identical with those of the product of the numbers.
$9 + 9 = 18$. $9 \times 9 = 81$.
$3 + 24 = 27$. $3 \times 24 = 72$.
$2 + 47 = 49$. $2 \times 47 = 94$.
$2 + 497 = 499$. $2 \times 497 = 994$.
$2 + 263 = 265$. $2 \times 263 = 526$.

■ How may three 7s be arranged so that they will equal 2?
$$\frac{7 + 7}{7} = 2.$$

■ What three consecutive numbers add up to 27?
$8 + 9 + 10 = 27$.

■ In what way can 1,000 be expressed as the sum of two or more consecutive numbers?
Here are three ways:
$198 + 199 + 200 + 201 + 202 = 1,000$.
$28 + 29 + 30 + 31 + 32 + 33 + 34 + 35 + 36 + 37 + 38 + 39 + 40 + 41 + 42 + 43 + 44 + 45 + 46 + 47 + 48 + 49 + 50 + 51 + 52 = 1,000$.
$55 + 56 + 57 + 58 + 59 + 60 + 61 + 62 + 63 + 64 + 65 + 66 + 67 + 69 + 70 = 1,000$.

■ Starting with a number made up of all the digits except 8 (12, 345, 679), select any digit as your key number. Multiply this digit by 9. Then multiply the original number by the product. The result will always be a number whose digits consist exclusively of your key number. See for yourself: Take 3 as your key number. $3 \times 9 = 27$. $12,345,679 \times 27 = 333,333,333$. If you take 4 as your key number, $4 \times 9 = 36$. $12,345,679 \times 36 = 444,444,444$.

■ Make a number consisting of all the digits from 1 through 9. Now make another number, reversing the order of the digits in the first number. Go through this process again. Add up all four numbers and add two. The result should be a number consisting exclusively of 2s.
See for yourself:

```
123,456,789
987,654,321
123,456,789
987,654,321
        + 2
222,222,222
```

■ Ask a friend to tell you his favorite number from 1 through 9. You then write two numbers on a piece of paper or a blackboard: 429 and 259. Have him multiply his favorite number by either of these two numbers, and then have him multiply the product by the other number. You can tell him in advance that the result will be a number whose digits consist exclusively of his favorite number.
The secret lies in the fact that the number 429, when multiplied by 259, has 111,111 as the product. $429 \times 259 = 111,111$. So any number that he multiplies this

product by will be repeated in the result. $2 \times 111,111 = 222,222.$ $5 \times 111,111 = 555,555.$

■ Start with any number having two or more digits. Rearrange the digits and subtract the smaller from the larger number. Your remainder will always be divisible by nine.
See for yourself: $83,457 - 75,843 = 7,614.$ $7,614 \div 9 = 846.$ $6,421 - 4,126 = 2,295.$ $2,295 \div 9 = 255.$

■ What number, when divided by 1, 2, 3, 4, 5, 6, 7, 8, 9, or 10, will always leave a remainder of 1?
2,521. See for yourself: $2,521 \div 2 = 1,262$ and a remainder 1. $2,521 \div 3 = 84$ and a remainder of 1.

■ Find two numbers whose difference and whose quotient are both equal to three.
The two numbers are $\frac{9}{2}$ and $\frac{3}{2}$. $9/2 - 3/2 = 6/2 = 3$; $9/2 \div 3/2 = 9/2 \times 2/3 = 3.$

■ Can you take one from four and leave five?
It's not impossible if you take one corner from a square. You will then have five corners left. See for yourself:

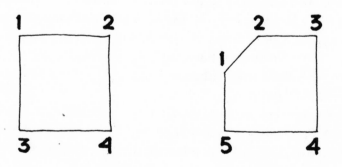

Here are some really freakish figures:

$$1 \times 9 + 2 = 11$$
$$12 \times 9 + 3 = 111$$
$$123 \times 9 + 4 = 1111$$
$$1234 \times 9 + 5 = 11111$$

Continuing to figure in this way will lead you to:
$$12345678 \times 9 + 9 = 111{,}111{,}111.$$

■ Give your answer quickly, without using pen or pencil: Which sum is the greater, that of the figures on the left or that of the figures on the right?

987654321	123456789
87654321	12345678
7654321	1234567
654321	123456
54321	12345
4321	1234
321	123
21	12
1	1

Believe it or not, they both add up to the same amount: 1,083,676,269. Do the additions and see for yourself!

■ Here's an oddity about the number 8:

$$9 \times 9 + 7 = 88$$
$$9 \times 98 + 6 = 888$$
$$9 \times 987 + 5 = 8888$$
$$9 \times 9876 + 4 = 88888$$
$$9 \times 98765 + 3 = 888888$$
$$9 \times 987654 + 2 = 8888888$$
$$9 \times 9876543 + 1 = 88888888$$
$$9 \times 98765432 + 0 = 888888888$$

■ And here's another oddity about the number 8:

$$1 \times 8 + 1 = 9$$
$$12 \times 8 + 2 = 98$$
$$123 \times 8 + 3 = 987$$
$$1234 \times 8 + 4 = 9876$$
$$12345 \times 8 + 5 = 98765$$
$$123456 \times 8 + 6 = 987654$$
$$1234567 \times 8 + 7 = 9876543$$
$$12345678 \times 8 + 8 = 98765432$$
$$123456789 \times 8 + 9 = 987654321$$

■ What is a *perfect number?* A perfect number is a number whose factors all add up to the original number. For example, 6 is a perfect number, because all of its factors (1, 2, and 3) add up to 6: $1 + 2 + 3 = 6$.
Another perfect number is 28. Its factors are 1, 2, 4, 7, and 14. $1 + 2 + 4 + 7 + 14 = 28$.

■ Using three digits of equal numerical value, express the number 30.
There are three ways of doing this: $33 - 3 = (5 \times 5) + 5 = 3^3 + 3 = 30$.

14

QUIPS AND JESTS

How does one overcome a child's distaste for arithmetic—
his feeling that it is a tedious task fraught with frus-
trations and worrisome difficulties?

By showing him that figures can be fun and by having
him associate numbers, counting, and calculating with
laughter. Arithmetic can be done not only without tears,
but with smiles and chuckles. Interjecting a little humor
in the form of a joke or a conundrum relieves the tension
that sometimes builds up when a youngster struggles
with sums, products, quotients, and remainders. He
relaxes, takes a "break" or a "breather"—we might say,
"jest for laughs"—and his spirits are lifted.

The pleasantries included in this chapter are to be
thought of as "spice," to be used sparingly to season
computations and to brighten the atmosphere in which
they are carried on.

■ Dad: Do you like math, son?
  Son: It's wonderful! I'm stuck on every problem.

■ Mother: What did you learn in arithmetic today?
  Child: Just gazintas!
  Mother: What's that?
  Child: You know, 2 gazinta 4, 4 gazinta 8 . . . .

■ When a lady faints, what number would revive her?
You must bring her 2.

■ What is the difference between 100 and 1,000?
Naught (0).

■ How would you add two numbers to 19 so that the
result is less than 20?
Add 1/2.

■ How much is $27 \times 94 \times 8 \times 0$?
0.

■ Three times what number is the same as eight times
what number?
3×0 is the same as 8×0.

■ In a field of 300 sheep, 3 shepherds, 2 horses, and 3
dogs, how many feet can you count?
Six feet; the others are hoofs and paws.

■ Mother: What mark did you get in math?
  Child: Underwater.
  Mother: What does that mean?
  Child: Below C level.

■ Add two strokes to the following number and make a man.

■ Draw six lines; then add five more to make nine.

| | | | | |

N I N E

■ Add two strokes and make nothing.

| | | |

N I X

■ A man gave a cashier a card with the number 102004180 and walked out the door. Why did he not have to pay?
Because it read: I ought to owe nothing, for I ate nothing.

By adding some lines we get

My favorite numbers are

OOOI IIIOIII
gOOD NIGHT

and

I I I I I I I I
TH E EN ☺

A FUTURE MATHEMATICIAN

Little boy Billy went into a candy store and asked, "How much are your candy sticks?"

The clerk answered, "Six for five cents."

Billy thought and said, "Six for five cents, five for four cents, four for three cents, three for two cents, two for one cent, and one for nothing. I'll take one, please."

■ Can you prove that $10 \times 2 = 11 \times 2$?

Ten times two equals twenty. Eleven times two equals twenty-two—that is, twenty too.

■ A butcher is six feet, two inches tall. What does he weigh?
Meat, of course!

■ Two fathers and two sons divided three dollars among them. Each of them received exactly one dollar. How was this possible?
There were only three people: grandfather, father, and son.

■ What gets larger the more you take from it?
A hole.

■ If you see twenty dogs running down the street, what time is it?
Nineteen after one.

■ If a father gives fifteen cents to his son and ten cents to his daughter, what time is it?
A quarter to two.

■ How much dirt is there in a hole a foot long, a foot wide, and a foot deep?
None.

■ How can you tell the score of a game *before* it begins?
Before a game begins, the score is always 0–0.

■ Which weighs more, a pound of feathers or a pound of gold?
A pound is a pound, you say, and so they both weigh the same?
No, you are wrong! A pound of feathers weighs more than a pound of gold.
How so?

Because a pound of feathers is sixteen ounces avoirdupois weight, whereas a pound of gold consists of only twelve ounces troy weight.

■ What has twelve feet but cannot walk?
Three yardsticks.

■ How many feet in a yard?
That depends on how many people are standing there.

■ What did one arithmetic book say to the other?
"I've got problems."

■ Did you see what happened to the plant in the mathematics class?
No, what?
It grew square roots.

■ How do you divide three apples among four people?
Make applesauce.

■ Are you good at addition?
Am I good at addition? I added this account up ten times. Here are the ten different answers.

■ Why are you taking those mathematics problems to the gymnasium?
I have to reduce these fractions.

■ If I tear a piece of paper into four pieces, what do I get?
Quarters.
And if I divide it eight times?
Eights.
And if I divide it into eight thousand parts?
Confetti.

■ Johnny, if your father could save one dollar a week for four weeks, what would he have?
A radio, a refrigerator, a new suit, and a lot more furniture.

■ Teacher: It is a pleasure for me to give you an 85 in mathematics.
   Student: Make it 100 and enjoy yourself.

■ If there are ten fingers on two hands, how many fingers are there on ten hands?
Not ten times ten, which equals one hundred, but only fifty (ten times five).

■ Why is a nickel smarter than a penny?
Because a nickel has more sense (cents).

■ Why is a lame dog like a boy adding 6 and 7?
He puts down three and carries one.

■ Why should 288 never be in refined company?
Because 288 is two gross.

■ Teacher: How many make a million?
   Johnny: Not many.

■ Teacher: How many peas are there in a pint?
   Mary: One *p*.

■ Which statement is correct: "Five and seven is eleven" or "Five and seven are eleven"?
Neither. $5 + 7 = 12$.

■ When do 2 and 2 make more than 4?
When they are written as 22.

■ Mother: Did you eat the cookies in the jar?
Boy: I didn't touch one.
Mother: But there's only one left.
Boy: That's the one I didn't touch.

■ What odd number becomes even when beheaded.
Seven becomes even.

■ What number becomes zero when beheaded.
8 becomes 0.

■ What's the difference between twice twenty-two and twice two and twenty?
Twenty. $2 \times 22 = 44$. $(2 \times 2) + 20 = 4 + 20 = 24$. $44 - 24 = 20$.

■ What is the process by which you cannot divide unless you multiply?
Cell division.

■ Can you prove that $6 \times 5 = 8 \times 4$?
$6 \times 5 = 30$. $8 \times 4 = 32$, that is, thirty too.

■ Can you prove that a bottle full equals a bottle empty.
A bottle 1/2 full = a bottle 1/2 empty.
Multiply both sides of the equation by 2.
Then, a bottle full = a bottle empty.

■ How many times can you subtract 10 from 100?
Only once. Every other subtraction is from a smaller number.

■ Why is Ireland likely to become the richest country in the world?
Because its capital is always Dublin.

■ How would you define a circle?
A circle is a round, fine line with no kinks in it, joined up so as not to show where it began.

■ What Roman numeral grows?
IV (ivy).

■ Show that two-thirds of six is nine.
Two-thirds of SIX is IX.

■ If next to a half dozen you place six, and then place five hundred next to it, the result is clear, lucid, glowing. How so?
VI is a half dozen. VI is six. D is a hundred. VIVID is lucid, clear, glowing.

■ What is a good way to remember Roman numeral values?
Just say, "I'm Very eXcited when Little Cats Drink Milk," and remember that

I = 1	C =	100
V = 5	D =	500
X = 10	M =	1,000
L = 50		

■ What's a polygon?
A dead parrot, of course.

■ Use the word "geometry" in a sentence.
A little acorn was planted in the ground. When it grew up, it said, "Geometry!" ("Gee! I'm a tree!")

■ What can be right, but never wrong?
An angle.

■ Place two buttons or coins in your hand, close your fist, and ask your friend, "How many things do I have in my hand?" You have made sure that he saw you take the two objects in your hand. His answer will be "two."

"No," you say; "there are three."

"But there are only two," he will object.

But you insist. "I say there are three. How much do you give if I'm wrong?"

"I'll give you a quarter."

"Well, then, hand over your quarter, because I'm wrong." And he will suddenly realize that you were right in being wrong!

■ What is the oldest table in the world?
The multiplication table.

■ Why is a calendar sad?
Because its days are numbered.

PART FOUR
APPENDIX

THE LANGUAGE OF ARITHMETIC

ADDITION (+): adding two or more numbers. The numbers to be added are the *addends*. The total of the addition is the *sum*. In $2 + 4 = 6$, the 2 and the 4 are addends, and the 6 is the sum.

SUBTRACTION (−): taking away a smaller number from a larger. The larger number is the *minuend;* the smaller number, the *subtrahend;* and the remainder is the *difference*. In $6 − 4 = 2$, 6 is the minuend, 4 is the subtrahend, and 2 is the difference.

MULTIPLICATION (×): adding a number to itself a number of times. The number to be multiplied is the *multiplicand;* the number of addends is the *multiplier;* and the total result of the addition is the *product*. In $318 \times 2 = 636$, 318 is the multiplicand, 2 is the multiplier, and 636 is the product.

DIVISION (÷): determining how many times one number is contained in another. The number to be divided is the *dividend;* the number by which the dividend is to be divided is the *divisor;* and the number of times the divisor is contained in the dividend is the *quotient*. In $4{,}368 \div 6 = 728$, 4,368 is the dividend, 6 is the divisor, and 728 is the quotient.

INVERSE: the opposite operation. Subtraction is the inverse of addition. Division is the inverse of multiplication.

FRACTION: a part of a unit or a quotient shown with the dividend above a horizontal line and the divisor below. The number written above the line is the *numerator;*

the number below the line is the *denominator*. In $\frac{1}{3}$, the 1 is the numerator, and the 3 is the denominator. A *proper fraction* is one in which the numerator is less than the denominator, indicating a part of a unit. 3/4 is a proper fraction. An *improper fraction* is one in which the denominator is less than the numerator. A *mixed number* is an *integer* (or whole number) combined with a proper fraction. 6 1/3 is a mixed number. To change a mixed number to an improper fraction, multiply the integer by the denominator of the fraction, add the product to the numerator, and use the original denominator. For example. to change 5 3/7 to an improper fraction, follow this procedure: $\dfrac{(5 \times 7) + 3}{7} = \dfrac{35 + 3}{7} = \dfrac{38}{7}$.

In a *simple fraction*, both the numerator and the denominator are integers. 7/8 is a simple fraction. In a *complex fraction*, either the numerator or the denominator or both are themselves fractions or mixed numbers. $\dfrac{1/3}{7}$, $\dfrac{7}{1/3}$, $\dfrac{1/2}{2/5}$, $\dfrac{5\,1/2}{6}$, $\dfrac{6}{5\,1/2}$, $\dfrac{7\,1/4}{6\,3/8}$ are all complex fractions.

RATIO (:): the quotient of one number divided by another of the same kind. The ratio of 2 to 3 may be written as 2:3 or as a fraction, $\frac{2}{3}$, or as a division 2 ÷ 3.

FACTOR: any one of the numbers which, when multiplied together, form a product. In 3 × 2 = 6, 3 and 2 are factors of 6. Other factors of 6 are 6 and 1.

DECIMAL: one or more integers placed to the right of a decimal point (.) representing a fraction, with each decimal place to the right of the decimal point indicating the equivalent multiple of one-tenth of the amount represented on its left. Thus, .2 = 2/10; .02 = 2/100; and .002 = 2/1000.

PERCENTAGE: a fraction with 100 as the denominator, formed by multiplying a decimal equivalent of a fraction by 100. For example, .25 is a percentage of 25 or 25 percent (that is, 25 per 100).

AREA: the number of square units in a surface. An area of 1 square inch is the space in a square 1" × 1". An area of a square foot is the space in a square 1' × 1'. An area of a square mile is the space enclosed in a square 1 mile long and 1 mile wide.

The difference in area between a 2-inch square and 2 square inches is 2 square inches. The area of a 2-inch square is 2" × 2" = 4 square inches. The area of 2 square inches is 2 square inches. So the difference is 2 square inches.

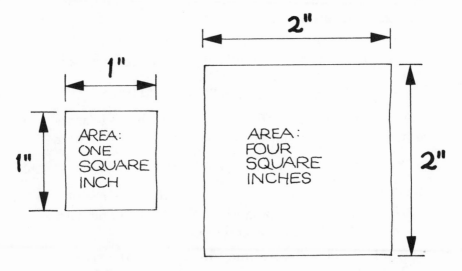

VOLUME: the number of cubic units in a solid figure, that is, one having three dimensions: length, width, and height. Thus, the volume of a solid 7 inches long, 3 inches wide, and 2 inches high is 7" × 3" × 2" = 42 cubic inches.

SQUARED NUMBER: a number multiplied by itself. For example, $3^2 = 3 \times 3 = 9$. The sign of the squaring of a number is the *exponent* 2, placed to the right of and above the number, indicating that the number is to be raised to the *second power*. Thus, $8^2 = 8 \times 8 = 64$.

PRIME NUMBER: a number that can be divided only by itself and by 1. For example, 7 is a prime number, since it is divisible only by 7 and by 1.

COMPOSITE NUMBER: a number that is the product of two or more integers each greater than 1.

SQUARE ROOT: a divisor of a number which is equal to the square of the divisor. Thus, 5 is the square root of 25 because $25 = 5^2 = 5 \times 5$. The number whose square root is to be indicated is placed under the symbol $\sqrt{}$. For example, $\sqrt{25} = 5$.

CUBED NUMBER: a number multiplied by itself three times or raised to the *third power*. The sign of the cubing of a number is the exponent 3, placed to the right of and above the number. Thus, $10^3 = 10 \times 10 \times 10 = 1{,}000$.

CUBE ROOT: a divisor of a number which is equal to the cube of the divisor. Thus, the number which, when multiplied by itself three times, has 64 as the product is the cube root of 64. $4 \times 4 \times 4 = 64$. The cube root of $64 = 4$. The number whose cube root is to be indicated is placed under the symbol $\sqrt[3]{}$. For example, $\sqrt[3]{125} = 5$, because $5 \times 5 \times 5 = 125$.

TABLE OF EQUIVALENTS

MEASUREMENTS

Liquid

2 pints (pts.)	= 1 quart (qt.)
4 quarts (qts.)	= 1 gallon (gal.)

Weight

16 ounces (oz.)	= 1 pound (lb.)
2,000 pounds (lbs.)	= 1 ton

Linear

12 inches (in.)	= 1 foot (ft.)
3 feet (ft.)	= 1 yard (yd.)
5,280 feet	= 1 mile

Time

60 seconds (secs.)	= 1 minute (min.)
60 minutes (mins.)	= 1 hour (hr.)
24 hours (hrs.)	= 1 day
7 days	= 1 week (wk.)
4 weeks (wks.)	= 1 month (mo.)
12 months (mos.)	= 1 year (yr.)
365 days	= 1 year
366 days	= 1 leap year
10 years (yrs.)	= 1 decade
100 years	= 1 century
1,000 years	= 1 millennium

Area

144 square inches	= 1 square foot (sq. ft.)
9 square feet	= 1 square yard (sq. yd.)

ROMAN NUMERALS	ARABIC NUMERALS
I, II, III, IV	= 1, 2, 3, 4
V, VI, VII, VIII	= 5, 6, 7, 8
IX, X, XI	= 9, 10, 11
XX, XXX	= 20, 30
XL, L, LX	= 40, 50, 60
XC, C, CX	= 90, 100, 110
CD, D, DC	= 400, 500, 600
CM, M, MC	= 900, 1,000, 1,100
MCMLXXIII	= 1973

COINS

1 cent	=	1¢ = $ .01
1 nickel	=	5¢ = .05
1 dime	=	10¢ = .10
1 quarter (dollar)	=	25¢ = .25
1 half (dollar)	=	50¢ = .50
1 dollar	=	100¢ = 1.00

FRACTIONS		DECIMALS
1/2	=	.50
1/3	=	.33 1/3
1/4	=	.25
1/5	=	.20
2/3	=	.66 2/3
3/4	=	.75
1/6	=	.16 2/3
5/6	=	.83 1/3
1/8	=	.12 1/2 = .125
3/8	=	.37 1/2 = .375
5/8	=	.62 1/2 = .625
7/8	=	.87 1/2 = .875
3/10	=	.30
7/10	=	.70
9/10	=	.90

OTHER BOOKS OF MATHEMATICAL GAMES

Adler, Irving. *Magic House of Numbers*. New York: John Day Co., 1957.

Asimov, Issac. *Quick and Easy Math*. Boston: Houghton Mifflin Co., 1964.

Beiler, Albert H. *Recreations in the Theory of Numbers — The Queen of Mathematics Entertains*. New York: Dover Publications, 1964.

Bendick, Jeanne, and Levin, Marcia. *Take Shapes, Lines, and Letters*. New York: McGraw Hill, Whittlesey House, 1965.

Crane, George W. *Test Your Horse Sense*. Chicago: Chicago Tribune, 1942.

Crescimbeni, Joseph. *Arithmetic Enrichment*. West Nyack, N.Y.: Parker Publishing, 1965.

Degrazia, Joseph. *Math Is Fun*. New York: Emerson Books, 1955.

Domoryad, A. P. *Math Games and Pastimes*. Elmsford, N.Y.: Macmillan Co., Pergamon, 1964.

Dumas, Enoch. *Arithmetic Games*. San Francisco: Fearon Publishers, 1971.

Feravolo, Poceo. *Wonders of Mathematics*. New York: Dodd, Mead, and Co., 1963.

Friend, J. Newton. *Fun, Numbers, and Facts*. New York: Charles Scribner's Sons, 1954.

Frolechstein, Jack. *Math Fun Games.* New York: Dover Publications, 1962.

Golomb, Solomon W. *Polyominoes: The Fascinating New Recreation in Mathematics.* New York: Charles Scribner's Sons, 1965.

Hartkopf, Roy. *Math Without Tears.* New York: Emerson Books, 1970.

Heafford, Philip. *The Math Entertainer.* New York: Emerson Books, 1959.

Hindman, Darwin A. *Complete Book of Games and Stunts.* Englewood Cliffs, N.J.: Prentice Hall, 1956.

Horne, Sylvia. *Patterns and Puzzles in Mathematics.* Chicago: Meredith Corp., 1970.

Johnson, Donovan A. *Games for Learning Arithmetic.* Portland, Me.: J. Weston Walch, 1960.

Jonas, Arthur. *More New Ways in Math.* Englewood Cliffs, N.J.: Prentice Hall, 1964.

Langman, Harry. *Play Mathematics.* New York: Hafner Publishing Co., 1962.

Leopold, Jules. *Check Your Wits!* New York: McGraw Hill, 1948.

Lieber, Lillian. *Take a Number.* Lancaster, Pa.: Jacques Caltell Press, 1946.

Meyer, Jerome S. *Fun for the Family.* New York: Garden City Publishing Co., 1939.

Meyer, Jerome S., and Hanlon, Stuart. *Fun with the New Math.* New York: Hawthorn Books, 1966.

Moore, William. *How Fast, How Far, How Much?* New York: G. P. Putnam's Sons, 1966.

Mott-Smith, Geoffrey. *Mathematical Puzzles.* rev. ed. New York: Dover Publications, 1954.

National Council of Teachers of Mathematics.
Enrichment Mathematics for the Grades. Washington,
D.C.: National Teacher Association,

O'Beirne, T. H. *Puzzles and Paradoxes*. New York:
Oxford University Press, 1965.

Razzell, Arthur G., and Watts, K. G. O. *Three and the
Shape of Three*. New York: Doubleday and Co., 1969.

Schadeler, Reuben A., and Leymour, Dale G.
Pic-a-Puzzle. Palo Alto, Calif.: Creative Publications,
1970.

Schuh, Fred. *The Master Book of Mathematical
Recreations*. New York: Dover Publications, 1968.

Simon, William. *Mathematical Magic*. New York:
Charles Scribner's Sons, 1964.

Tedfore, Jack. *The Giant Book of Family Fun and
Games*. New York: Franklin Watts, 1958.

Thomas, Janet K. *Teaching Arithmetic to Mentally
Retarded Children*. Minneapolis, Minn.: T. S. Denison
and Co., 1968.

COMMERCIALLY AVAILABLE ARITHMETIC GAMES

This compilation of commercial games is included for
parents and teachers who want to supplement the games
in the book. The listed games are of various levels of

difficulty and quality. However, in the opinion of the authors each game has some element that makes it educational and enjoyable. Several, particularly Tuf, use materials such as cards, cubes, dice, dominoes, and spinners that are also called for by some of the games in this book.

ADD-A-GRAMS   Number blocks and plus blocks to be arranged to produce sums. Palfreys School Supply Co. (7715 East Garvey Boulevard, South San Gabriel, California).

ADDI-FAX   A card game for addition. Another, called *Multi-fax,* teaches multiplication, and a third, called *Fracti-fax,* teaches the decimal and percentage equivalents of fractions. Plaway Games.

ADDO AND MULTO   Card games played like Bingo with problems in addition and multiplication. Kenworthy Educational Service, Inc. (138 Allen Street, Buffalo, New York).

ARITHMETIC DOMINOES   Practice in counting, adding, reading numbers. Arithmetic Clinic (4502 Stanford Street, Chevy Chase, Maryland).

ARITHO   A card game played like Bingo. Psychological Service (4402 Stanford Street, Chevy Chase, Maryland).

BRAINIAC   Construction kit for building small electronic "brain" that computes and solves problems. Berkeley Enterprises.

CILAMP GAMES   Teaches all arithmetical operations. Midwestern Paper Company (1801 Hull Avenue, Des Moines, Iowa).

COMBINATIONS ARE FUN   Teaches addition. Kenworthy Educational Service, Inc. (138 Allen Street, Buffalo, New York).

ELECTRIC QUIZBOOK Electrical device flashes a light when question and answer are touched simultaneously. Models of Industry, Inc. (2100 Fifth Street, Berkeley, California).

EQUATIONS Players try to make equations with symboled cubes and to prevent opponents from doing so. Science Research Associates, Inc. (259 East Erie Street, Chicago, Illinois).

FRACTION FUN Fractional parts of a circle involving different denominators to be added to make a whole circle. Palfreys School Supply Co. (7715 East Garvey Boulevard, South San Gabriel, California).

FUN WITH NUMBERS Eighteen decks of twenty-five cards each, graded in difficulty, involving matching of answers to problems in arithmetic. Exclusive Playing Card Company (1139 South Wabash Avenue, Chicago, Illinois).

GINN GAMES Teaches all operations of arithmetic. Ginn and Company (Boston, Massachusetts).

HIT Teaches multiplication and division. As many as twenty-five can play. Plaway Games.

IMMA WHIZ A Bingo game that teaches all operations of arithmetic. Kenworthy Educational Service, Inc. (138 Allen Street, Buffalo, New York).

IMOUT A spinning game like Bingo that teaches all operations with whole numbers and fractions. Imout (P. O. Box 1944, Cleveland, Ohio).

JUNIOR EXECUTIVE Teaches the mathematics of business practice: profits, interest, percentages, etc. Western Publishing Company, Inc. (1220 Mound Avenew, Racine, Wisconsin).

KRECT Card game that teaches fractions, percentages, decimal equivalents, and all arithmetical operations.

Self-Teaching Flashers (4402 South 54 Street, Lincoln, Nebraska).

LOTTO   Teaches number recognition. E. S. Fairchild Corporation (Rochester, New York).

LOTTO GAME   Designed for four players, this card game teaches multiplication. Cuisenaire Company of America (246 East 46th Street, New York, New York).

MAKE ONE   Fraction and percent cards are combined to "make one" in the form of a whole circle. Garrard Press (510 North Hickory Street, Champaign, Illinois).

MATH MAGIC   A five-in-one game that provides drill in the fundamental operations of arithmetic with dice, cards, and spinners. Cadaco-Ellis, Inc. (310 West Polk Street, Chicago, Illinois).

MATRIX   Board, markers, and indicators teach strategy. King Enterprises (New City, Rockland County, New York).

MY ARITHMETIC TEACHER   Pegs are put in holes to indicate answers to problems involving all arithmetical operations. Arithmetic Clinic (4502 Stanford Street, Chevy Chase, Maryland).

NUMBER FUN   Interlocking cardboard tiles with numbers are arranged to solve problems. Palfreys School Supply Company (7715 East Garvey Boulevard, South San Gabriel, California).

NUMBERLAND SPECIAL   Answers to problems in arithmetic in the form of children, cattle, autos. *Old Woman in the Shoe* teaches subtraction; *Parking Lot,* multiplication; and *Round-up,* division — all by similar means. Ideal School Supply Company (8312 Birkhoff Avenue, Chicago, Illinois).

NUMBLE   A cross number game. Selchow and Righter Company (2215 Union Boulevard, Bay Shore, New York).

ON SET   Thirty different games, like Equations, to teach the basic ideas of set theory. Wff 'N Proof Learning Games Associates (1111 Maple Avenue, Turtle Creek, Pennsylvania).

PRIMARY NUMBER CARDS   Numbers and patterns on cardboard to be cut into cards for testing addition. Hall and McCreary Company.

QUIZMO   Bingo game teaching all arithmetical operations with whole numbers and fractions. Milton Bradley Company (74 Park Street, Springfield, Massachusetts).

REAL NUMBER GAME   Dice game teaching number formation. Wff 'N Proof Learning Games Associates (1111 Maple Avenue, Turtle Creek, Pennsylvania).

SAY-IT   Played like Lotto, this game teaches all arithmetical operations. Garrard Press (510 North Hickory Street, Champaign, Illinois).

SCOR-O   Number blocks to teach all arithmetical operations. Champion Publishing Company (612 North Second Street, St. Louis, Missouri).

SELF-TEACHING FLASHERS   Flash cards that teach all arithmetical operations for three to ten players. Self-Teaching Flashers (4402 South 54 Street, Lincoln, Nebraska).

SPINNER FRACTION PIE   Also in the form of *Spinner Fraction Squares*. Rubber fraction pies or squares cut in halves, thirds, fourths, etc., to make wholes after being selected by a spinner. Creative Playthings (Herndon, Pennsylvania).

SPINNO   Dials with problems and answers involving all arithmetical operations. John C. Winston Company (1010 Arch Street, Philadelphia, Pennsylvania).

THIRTEEN   Played like Scrabble with numbered tiles and a board to teach addition and multiplication.

Cadaco-Ellis, Inc. (310 West Polk Street, Chicago, Illinois).

TIMES SQUARE   Played like Bingo, this can be combined or joined to *Divvy-up, Add-a-Lad,* and *Anchors Away,* to teach all arithmetical operations. Kraeg Games (8988 Manchester Avenue, St. Louis, Missouri).

TUF   Numbered and symboled dice are used to form equations. Tuf (P.O. Box 173, Rowayton, Connecticut).

UPSIDE-DOWN ARITHMETIC   Disks, spinner, and lattice-board used to teach multiplication and division. Jeff's Arithmetic Games (2900 S.W. 71 Street, Miami, Florida).

INDEX
OF SKILLS TAUGHT

ADDITION

Addition Magician, 179; Add-Joining Cards, 77;
A-Lotto-Numbers, 163; A-Rhythm-e-Tag, 143;
Arithme-Tic-Tac-Toe, 50; Banker, 114; Baseball Mads, 89,
Batter Up! 157; Boxing Match, 154;
Case of the Missing Number, The, 174; Casino Baseball, 88;
Coin Count, 39; Coin Toss, 147; Color Me Mad, 19; Color Me Sad, 17;
Combinations, 131; Concentration, 91; Configurations, 53;
Contact, 110; Count Down, 24; Crisscross, 51; Cross Out, 30;
Division Precision, 173; Drop It! 138; Exact Card, The, 175;
Exact Measure, 130; Exact Reckoning, 128; Exact Weight, 129;
Finger Figures, 44; Finger Shoot, 46; Fireman up the Ladder, 94;
Flip-Count, 72; Follow the Numbers, 22; Fraction Blackjack, 72;
Giant Step, 141; Give and Take, 74; Golf, 107; Handy Figures, 40;
High-Low, 121; Imprisoned Numbers, 59; I've Got Your Number! 25;
Line-Up, 126; Locus Pocus, 104; Mads Bingo, 162;
Mads Dominoes, 119; Mads Pyramid, 66; Mads War, 69; Make It, 38;
Marble Pitch, 145; Math Path, 98; Multisum, 82; Numbered Daze, 29;
Number-Ring Toss, 148; Number Row, 53; Number Twirl, 31;
Odds and Evens, 171; Odd or Even, 172; Pitch and Toss, 28;
Pitch or Snap, 27; Poker Dice, 115; Precise Dice, 93;
Precise Word, The, 176; Psychic Arithmetic, 170; Pyramid, 63;
Sad Casino, 85; Sam Pyramid, 66; Sets and Sequences, 83;
Six Clicks, 116; Snatch-a-Batch, 42; Snatch Match, 41;
Some Sums! 61; Square Accounts, 56; Sum Bingo, 161;
Sum Building, 63; Sum Mystery, 168; Sum Speed, 166; Tag, 132;
Target 15, 26; Target 31, 80; Tic-Tac Bingo, 67; Trail Blazing, 96;
Trial and Error, 33; 29 Game, 78; Unboxing Match, 156;
What Are the Odds? 178; Your Number's Up! 160

ASSOCIATING NUMBERS WITH FACTS

Number, Please, 34

CONVERTING EQUIVALENT VALUES

Batter Up! 157; Boxing Match, 154; Coin Count, 39;
Decimal Designs, 113; Drop It! 138; Exact Measure, 130;

Exact Weight, 129; Fraction Extraction, 113; Handy Figures, 40;
Number, Please, 34; Snatch-a-Batch, 42; Snatch Match, 41;
Unboxing Match, 156

COUNTING

Buzz, 36; Count and Connect, 19; Count Down, 24; Flip-Count, 73;
Hippety-Hop Buzz, 38; Number Maze, 48; Sets and Sequences, 83;
Umpty-Um Buzz, 38; War, 68; What's the Difference? 43;
Write Connections, 21

DECIMAL OPERATIONS

A-Rhythm-e-Tag, 143; Banker, 114; Batter Up! 157;
Boxing Match, 154; Decimal Designs, 113; Fraction Extraction, 113;
Giant Step, 141; Number Twirl, 31; Unboxing Match, 156

DISTINGUISHING BETWEEN GREATER AND LESS

Back Numbers, 145; Fraction Blackjack, 72; Fraction War, 70;
I've Got Your Number! 25; War, 68; What's My Number? 158;
Your Number's Up! 160

DISTINGUISHING BETWEEN ODD AND EVEN NUMBERS

Back Numbers, 145; Crisscross, 51; Follow the Numbers, 22;
I've Got Your Number! 25; Number Maze, 48;
What Are the Odds? 178; Your Number's Up! 160

DISTINGUISHING BETWEEN PRIME
AND COMPOSITE NUMBERS

Follow the Numbers, 22; Number Maze, 48

DIVISION

A-Lotto-Numbers, 163; A-Rhythm-e-Tag, 143; Back Numbers, 145;
Banker, 114; Baseball Mads, 89; Batter Up! 157; Boxing Match, 154;
Buzz, 36; Casino Baseball, 88; Coin Toss, 147; Color Me Mad, 19;
Color Me Sad, 17; Combinations, 131; Contact, 110;
Digital Computer, 45; Divide and Conquer, 153;
Division Precision, 173; Divisor Deviser, 133; Drop It! 138;
Exact Reckoning, 128; Factor Extractor, 112; Factor Hockey, 135;
Finger Shoot, 46; Gazintas, 46; Giant Step, 141; Golf, 107;
Handy Figures, 40; Hippety-Hop Buzz, 38; I've Got Your Number! 25;
Mads Bingo, 162; Mads Dominoes, 119; Mads Pyramid, 66;
Mads War, 69; Make It, 38; Math Path, 98; Multisum, 82;
Number-Ring Toss, 148; Poker Dice, 115; Precise Word, The, 176;
Product Net, 55; Sad Casino, 85; Snake, The, 98; Snatch-a-Batch, 42;
Snatch Match, 41; Table Numbers, 75; Tag, 132; Target 31, 80;
Trial and Error, 33; Umpty-Um Buzz, 38; Unboxing Match, 156;
Your Number's Up! 160

FACTORING

Back Numbers, 145; Divisor Deviser, 133; Exact Reckoning, 128;
Factor Extractor, 112; Factor Hockey, 135; Product Net, 55

FRACTION OPERATIONS

A-Rhythm-e-Tag, 143; Batter Up! 157; Boxing Match, 154;
Drop It! 138; Exact Measure, 130; Exact Weight, 129;
Fraction Blackjack, 72; Fraction Extraction, 113; Fraction War, 70;
Giant Step, 141; Unboxing Match, 156; Your Number's Up! 160

MAKING CHANGE

Banker, 114; Coin Count, 39

MULTIPLICATION

Add-Joining Cards, 77; A-Lotto-Numbers, 163; A-Rhythm-e-Tag, 143;
Banker, 114; Baseball Mads, 89; Batter Up! 157; Boxing Match, 154;
Buzz, 36; Casino Baseball, 88; Coin Count, 39; Coin Toss, 147;
Color Me Mad, 19; Combinations, 131; Concentration, 91;
Configurations, 53; Contact, 110; Count and Connect, 19;
Cross Out, 30; Digital Computer, 45; Divisor Deviser, 133;
Drop It! 138; Exact Card, The, 175; Exact Reckoning, 128;
Factor Extractor, 112; Factor Hockey, 135; Finger Shoot, 46;
Gazintas, 46; Giant Step, 141; Golf, 107; Handy Figures, 40;
Hippety-Hop Buzz, 38; Imprisoned Numbers, 59;
I've Got Your Number! 25; Locus Pocus, 104; Mads Bingo, 162;
Mads Dominoes, 119; Mads Pyramid, 66; Mads War, 69; Make It, 38;
Marble Pitch, 145; Math Path, 98; Multisum, 82; Numbered Daze, 29;
Number-Ring Toss, 148; Number Twirl, 31; Odds and Evens, 171;
Pitch and Toss, 28; Pitch or Snap, 27; Poker Dice, 115;
Precise Dice, 93; Precise Word, The, 176; Product Net, 55;
Sam Pyramid, 66; Sets and Sequences, 83; Snatch-a-Batch, 42;
Snatch Match, 41; Stand Up and Be Counted, 150;
Table Numbers, 75; Tag, 132; Target 31, 80; Tic-Tac Bingo, 67;
Trial and Error, 33; Umpty-Um Buzz, 38; Unboxing Match, 156;
Write Connections, 21; Your Number's Up! 160

PLOTTING POINTS ON A GRAPH

Golf, 107; Line-Up, 126; Locus Pocus, 104; Sink the Ship, 102

RECOGNIZING AND IDENTIFYING GEOMETRIC FIGURES

Figure It Out, 123

RECOGNIZING NUMERALS

Color Me, 16

RECOGNIZING ROMAN NUMERALS

Batter Up! 157; Boxing Match, 154; Pitch or Snap, 27

RECOGNIZING SETS

Poker Dice, 115; Sets and Sequences, 83

RECOGNIZING SQUARES, CUBES, ETC.

Divisor Deviser, 133

SUBTRACTION

A-Lotto-Numbers, 163; A-Rhythm-e-Tag, 143;
Arithme-Tic-Tac-Toe, 50; Banker, 114; Baseball Mads, 89;
Batter Up! 157; Boxing Match, 154;
Case of the Missing Number, The, 174; Casino Baseball, 88;
Coin Toss, 147; Color Me Sad, 17; Combinations, 131;
Configurations, 53; Contact, 110; Crisscross, 51;
Division Precision, 173; Drop It! 138; Exact Card, The, 175;
Exact Measure, 130; Exact Reckoning, 128; Exact Weight, 129;
Finger Figures, 44; Finger Shoot, 46; Fireman up the Ladder, 94;
Flip-Count, 73; Fraction Blackjack, 72; Giant Step, 141;
Give and Take, 74; Golf, 107; Handy Figures, 40; High-Low, 121;
Imprisoned Numbers, 59; I've Got Your Number, 25; Mads Bingo, 162;
Mads Dominoes, 119; Mads Pyramid, 66; Mads War, 69; Make It, 38;
Math Path, 98; Number-Ring Toss, 148; Number Row, 53;
Pitch and Toss, 28; Poker Dice, 115; Precise Dice, 93;
Precise Word, The, 176; Psychic Arithmetic, 170; Sad Casino, 85;
Sam Pyramid, 66; Snatch-a-Batch, 42; Snatch Match, 41;
Square Accounts, 56; Sum Speed, 166; Tag, 132; Target 31, 80;
Trail Blazing, 96; Trial and Error, 33; Unboxing Match, 156;
Use Twos, 119; What Are the Odds? 178; Won by One, 118;
Your Number's Up! 160

INDEX OF GAMES

Addition Magician, 179
Add-Joining Cards, 77
A-Lotto-Numbers, 163
A-Rhythm-e-Tag, 143
Arithme-Tic-Tac-Toe, 50

Back Numbers, 145
Banker, 114
Baseball Mads, 89
Batter Up! 157
Boxing Match, 154
Buzz, 36

Case of the Missing Number,
    The, 174
Casino Baseball, 88
Coin Count, 39
Coin Toss, 147
Color Me, 16
Color Me Mad, 19
Color Me Sad, 17
Combinations, 131
Concentration, 91
Configurations, 53
Contact, 110
Count and Connect, 19
Count Down, 24
Crisscross, 51
Cross Out, 30

Decimal Designs, 113
Digital Computer, 45
Divide and Conquer, 153
Division Precision, 173
Divisor Deviser, 133
Drop It! 138

Exact Card, The, 175
Exact Measure, 130
Exact Reckoning, 128
Exact Weight, 129

Factor Extractor, 112
Factor Hockey, 135

Figure It Out, 123
Finger Figures, 44
Finger Shoot, 46
Fireman up the Ladder, 94
Flip-Count, 73
Follow the Numbers, 22
Fraction Blackjack, 72
Fraction Extraction, 113
Fraction War, 70

Gazintas, 46
Giant Step, 141
Give and Take, 74
Golf, 107

Handy Figures, 40
High-Low, 121
Hippety-Hop Buzz, 38

Imprisoned Numbers, 59
I've Got Your Number! 25

Line-Up, 126
Locus Pocus, 104

Mads Bingo, 162
Mads Dominoes, 119
Mads Pyramid, 66
Mads War, 69
Make It, 38
Marble Pitch, 145
Math Path, 98
Multisum, 82

Numbered Daze, 29
Number Maze, 48
Number, Please, 34
Number-Ring Toss, 148
Number Row, 53
Number Twirl, 31

Odds and Evens, 171
Odd or Even? 172

Pitch and Toss, 28
Pitch or Snap, 27
Poker Dice, 115
Precise Dice, 93
Precise Word, The, 176
Product Net, 55
Psychic Arithmetic, 170
Pyramid, 63

Sad Casino, 85
Sam Pyramid, 66
Sets and Sequences, 83
Sink the Ship, 102
Six Clicks, 116
Snake, The, 98
Snatch-a-Batch, 42
Snatch Match, 41
Some Sums! 61
Square Accounts, 56
Stand Up and Be Counted, 150
Sum Bingo, 161
Sum Building, 63
Sum Mystery, 168
Sum Speed, 166

Table Numbers, 75
Tag, 132
Target 15, 26
Target 31, 80
Tic-Tac Bingo, 67
Trail Blazing, 96
Trial and Error, 33
29 Game, 78

Umpty-Um Buzz, 38
Unboxing Match, 156
Use Twos, 119

War, 68
What Are the Odds? 178
What's My Number? 158
What's the Difference? 43
Won by One, 118
Write Connections, 21

Your Number's Up! 160